42 Rules for Working Moms

Edited by Laura Lowell

SUPERSTAR press

E-mail: info@superstarpress.com
20660 Stevens Creek Blvd., Suite 210
Cupertino, CA 95014

First Printing: June 2008
Second Printing: November 2008
Paperback ISBN: 0-9799428-4-5 (978-0-9799428-4-6)
Place of Publication: Silicon Valley, California, USA
Library of Congress Number: 2008928151

eBook ISBN: 0-9799428-5-3 (978-0-9799428-5-3)

Trademarks

All terms mentioned in this book that are known to be trademarks or service marks have been appropriately capitalized. Super Star Press™ cannot attest to the accuracy of this information. Use of a term in this book should not be regarded as affecting the validity of any trademark or service mark.

Warning and Disclaimer

This book is a compilation of thoughts, ideas and opinions designed to provide insight and commentary on best practices in working motherhood. You are urged to talk to other working moms and tailor the information to your individual needs. For more information, you can always visit the website at http://42rules.com/working_moms.

Every effort has been made to make this book as complete and as accurate as possible, but no warranty of fitness is implied. The information provided is on an "as is" basis. The author, contributors, and publisher shall have neither liability nor responsibility to any person or entity with respect to any loss or damages arising from the information contained in the book.

If you do not wish to be bound by the above, you may return this book to the publisher for a full refund.

Publisher

- Mitchell Levy
  http://happyabout.info/

Executive Editor

- Laura Lowell
  http://superstarpress.com/

Cover Designer

- Cate Calson
  http://calsongraphics.com/

Layout

- Teclarity
  http://teclarity.com/

Dedication

To my mom Sharon, my Auntie Pam and my other mother Berta: You taught me how to be a great working mom without even knowing it. It is because of you, I am who I am. Thank you.

Acknowledgments

I want to personally and publicly thank all the wonderful moms who found a few extra hours in their already ridiculously busy lives to contribute to this book. Your involvement has proven that moms, working or not, are always ready and willing to give their hearts, minds, and souls to something they believe in.

I also want to acknowledge the over-the-top contributions of a few moms without whom this book wouldn't have happened.

Kelli Glass for being my editor (again) and fixing the same mistakes (again).

Pamela Castellanos for being the best friend, sister, mother, and wife I've ever known.

Amy Keroes for taking the time to help me see the true potential in this book and my vision for the rest.

An ode to working moms

Anita Lobo is a working mom with two kids (ages six and three) who advises multinational companies about the "India opportunity." She became the CEO of a boutique public relations agency when she was expecting her first child.

Women, be proud of who you are—
A woman, a mom, a corporate warrior
You have tried. You have made your mark
On the world's future.

I know it was tough
Proving yourself in the beginning,
But being a working mom,
Has brought life a new meaning.

Strive on, dear mom,
The world awaits your song.
Sing loud and clear,
Tell more women, they won't go wrong.

It's possible to successfully be
A great working mom
In this giant parody.

Contents

Contents

My fears have always revealed themselves to me through dreams. I am terrified of heights—so I have dreams of free-falling off the Golden Gate Bridge. I am afraid of being unprepared—so, when I was in school, I had recurring nightmares about having to take a final exam in a class I never attended. Now that I am a working mother of two, the dreams reveal my fears of parental inadequacy. You don't need a degree or even a passing grade to raise a child, so every parent at times feels utterly unqualified for the daunting responsibility of protecting and shaping the lives of their children. Working mothers have the additional fear that their time away will irreparably harm their children.

In this age of helicopter parenting, are we short-changing our children because other mothers are by their children's sides, coaching them to be better people during the hours we are, by choice or necessity, working? That was my fear for the first few years as a working parent. I did my best to be a productive professional and a present parent. I worried, I cried, I felt very, very guilty.

When my son was around three, I joined him for lunch at his day care. Most of the kids in his class were children of working parents. On that particular day, when it was time to leave, I told my son that I had to go back to work. One by one, from behind their sippy cups, each kid announced excitedly that their mommies had offices, too. Some said their mommies had computers; some said their moms had spinny chairs; some said their moms had pictures they had drawn on their desks. Whether they knew it or not, this unbridled enthusiasm was actually pride in their mothers' professional lives. For me that pride also gave me permission—permission to transform my fear of parental failure into something far more positive. Since that day, my working-mom fears have been converted into a courageous conviction that while I may very well mess up my kids—it will not be simply because I have a job.

Sadly, this epiphany did not alleviate the overwhelming challenges of my dual life. As founder and CEO of a Web site dedicated to informing and entertaining working moms, and as the working mother of two, I am keenly aware of our collective need for a rulebook to guide us as we attempt to tackle the daily tug-of-war between work and home.

42 Rules for Working Moms is the instruction manual we have all been waiting for. Finally, we have a resource capturing the best tips, tricks of the trade, and survival strategies from smart, savvy, supportive working moms. Consider this your map for making work—work. If you heed the creative and constructive advice set forth in this very inspired book, you will be well on your way to conquering the chaos of working mother-hood.

Amy Keroes is Founder and President of http://mommytrackd.com, a popular online magazine offering busy stay-at-work moms something they desperately need—a fresh, funny and helpful resource to help them manage the chaos of working motherhood. Amy is also the author of "Mom's Ultimate Family Organizer: A One Stop Planner for Busy Moms." Before starting Mommy Track'd, Amy was Senior Corporate Counsel for Gap Inc. She lives in Mill Valley, California, with her husband and two children.

Introduction

When I had my first daughter and returned to work six months later, I was very optimistic about my ability to "do it all." Today, after eight years as a working mom, I'm still optimistic, but I'm much more pragmatic about the whole thing. I can do it all, just not all at the same time.

The idea for this book was born out of experiences with my kids, my husband, and my girl friends—some who work outside the home and some who work just as hard (if not harder) at home. We're all working moms. The only difference is that some of us get paid in cash, and others get paid in kisses.

There have been studies that looked at the difference between families with two working parents, one working parent, single parent families, etc. There is little to no evidence of any significant difference one way or the other. We work for different reasons; to support our families, to contribute to the greater good, for the personal satisfaction or the financial rewards. Regardless of why we work, we all love our kids, and we do the best we can.

When my kids started school, I met lots of other moms, working and stay-at-home. I struggled with how to describe my role. I worked full-time from home. I took the kids to school and chatted with the "stay at homes" and volunteered in the classroom because I had a lot of flexibility. But both my husband and I had to work. That meant no chatting at the coffee shop at 10 a.m., no play dates, and the dreaded day care.

The contributors to this book have all dealt with these issues and more. They share their experiences, ideas, and opinions so that others like them can learn from their mistakes and benefit from the years of collected wisdom. As you read through the rules, I ask only one thing. Don't take them literally. In fact, don't even read them in order.

Feel free to pass them along to a Mom in need of a friendly little reminder. I invite you to share your "rules" and be part of an ongoing discussion. After all, these are our rules. What are yours?

1 Rules Are Meant To Be Broken

Rules can be bent, stretched, and even broken.

What keeps me sane, might make you crazy. What you think is heaven, might be my personal version of hell. It is the same with working motherhood.

The ideas of the contributors to this book are just that, their ideas, opinions and experiences. What works for them, might be just the thing you have been looking for, or you might give it a try and think to yourself, "What was she thinking?"

This was exactly what I thought at 2 a.m. one morning, while surfing a chat room for moms who couldn't get their kids to sleep. My daughter was about 9 months old. I had returned to work full-time and hadn't had a full night's sleep since she was born—an all too familiar tale. I read every book I could on "How to get your child to sleep"—everything from "cry it out" to "silent return to sleep" to the "family bed." Nothing worked for us. I was on chat rooms and bulletin boards. I was a wreck, my husband was a wreck, and our daughter could have cared less. She was only nine months old and would take two or three naps during the day.

I went to the pediatrician. He gave me a big hug, asked me how I was doing, and I began sobbing—again, an all too familiar tale. I explained what was going on, and the first words out of his mouth were, "Stop reading all that stuff."

His point was that everyone has different opinions. You know your child, your family and yourself. Take the ideas that make sense to you and give them a try. If they work, great; if not, chuck 'em out and try something else.

When my daughter moved into her "big-girl" bed, I decided it was better for everyone if I just lay down with her. It only took a few minutes, and she was sound asleep. The only problem was, most nights so was I. I'd wake up in her bed at 10:30 p.m., and the evening was gone. I had done nothing on my "list of things to do when she is asleep." Hrumpf.

When my second daughter was born, I was ecstatic. She was healthy and happy. Selfishly, I was looking forward to applying the lessons I learned with our first daughter. I wouldn't make the same mistakes twice, I confidently told myself. Indeed, I'd make a whole new set of mistakes. Hrumpf.

What I have learned is that there are no absolutes. Nothing works for everyone. We all have different styles, different personalities, and different idiosyncrasies. Take my sister and me. I am a very organized, schedule-driven person. That is how I approach life—including parenting. My kids had schedules, and we didn't mess with the schedules. As a result, I'm now trying to teach them about flexibility and how to "go with the flow." My sister is very intuitive and takes things as they come. Her kids have schedules too, but they are different from mine. They are not early morning people and tend to stay up later in the evenings. She manages quite well, and her kids are happy and well-adjusted. We're just different.

The ideas in this book are shared with the best of intentions. Some may work for you; others may not. You can take the ideas behind the rule and do with them what you will. They don't have to be followed to the letter. In fact, they can be bent, stretched, and even broken. The point is to learn from others, see what they do, get a good idea, and see what happens. You never know when a great idea might sneak up on you and make life as a working mom just a little bit easier.

2 Your Daughter Can Brush Her Own Hair

"When they get old enough to care what their hair looks like, they will brush it."

Robin Wolaner founded Parenting magazine in 1987 and sold the property to Time Inc., where she served as CEO of Sunset Publishing. She is the author of "Naked in the Boardroom: A CEO Bares Her Secrets So You Can Transform Your Career" and recently founded TeeBeeDee, http://www.tbd.com, a networking site for people over 40.

Maintenance is time-consuming. As a working mother, I gave up on regular manicures. It was enough to keep my hair looking professional (and, later, not gray). As soon as I could, I abandoned skirts for the same reason (keeping a supply of un-snagged pantyhose is beyond me).

While I could cheerily make trade-offs for myself, at first I had deep pangs when I would see other children beautifully dressed, with the boys' hair trimmed neatly and the girls' tresses arrayed with barrettes, braids, etc. I had given up on the idea that my kids' grooming reflected on me. I rationalized by saying that if they didn't brush their teeth twice a day, they would have to suffer the consequences. The theory was that not-nagging my kids would help them develop self-discipline. But, the real reason was, I couldn't do everything. (I'm terrible with a blow-dryer; my own style is wash-and-wear by necessity.)

In all seriousness, as the founder of *Parenting Magazine*, I do feel a bit responsible for the generation of "helicopter parents" who hover over their kids, feeling their successes as our own. If my (not-fully-employed) friend's daughter doesn't get into Harvard, my friend will be more devastated than her daughter. This begins early. Non-working mothers spend time competing with other mothers for the best-dressed kid, the best lunch packed for school, the fullest roster of lessons to which they drive their children. Working mothers are already competing in the office and don't have the time to compete in the lunchbox.

I think we, working mothers, are better off for this. While I am as competitive as the next person, I think it's fortunate that our lack of time saves us from the ugliness of getting our "wins" through our children's appearance and performance. We may pay a price in guilt, at the visible shame that our daughters don't have perfect hair or our sons wear wrinkled clothes, but those kids are taught a good lesson about taking care of themselves.

Yet, it's still hard to let go of the visible signs of a pampered child. The sooner a working mother can stop feeling responsible for every aspect of her child's life, the sooner that child can develop the resilience and self-sufficiency that will empower him later in life.

"When they get old enough to care what their hair looks like, they will brush it." This was a favorite saying of Leslie Jacobs, the founder of a large insurance agency whom I interviewed for my book, *Naked in the Boardroom: A CEO Bares Her Secrets So You Can Transform Your Career* (Simon & Schuster, 2005).

I don't want to gender-stereotype, as I'm sure there is an act of personal grooming equivalent to hair-brushing that we mothers do for our sons; in my case, being Jewish, circumcision was almost a foregone (no pun intended) conclusion. But the thought did occur to me that future nagging of my then-infant to keep clean would be one less thing on my list.

3 Stand Up Straight

Good posture is an important step in balancing the burdens of life!

Regan MacPherson is a single mom of a wonderful daughter, a pug and a cat, and is a full-time corporate attorney for a storage technology company in Silicon Valley.

The other morning, I was dressing for work, feeding the dog, doing laundry, and making my daughter's lunch. I leaned down to put on a pair of heels and felt a sharp ache in my back. The advice of my granny, who, while I was growing up, would frequently come up behind me, smack me between the shoulder blades, and issue the stern command "stand up straight!" reverberated loudly in my head.

I straightened up, put my shoulders back, and took a deep breath. I opted that day for a pair of flats. By paying attention to my posture that day, by the next, I was back in the proverbial saddle.

As working moms, we carry many loads, both literally and figuratively. We lug around our babies, our toddlers, and sometimes even our school-aged kids. We carry groceries and load after load of laundry; we mop floors and scrub toilets; and cook gourmet meals. We take care of our kids when they are sick or heartsick, bored or delighted. We care for the family pets and often for a spouse or elderly parent. We keep family relations intact with our own siblings and parents, and sometimes our in-laws.

As employees, we carry a different load. We lug our laptops and other work-related items back and forth between meetings. We manage relationships with our bosses, employees, and co-workers. We carry the emotional weight of financially supporting a family. At the end of the day, after helping the kids with homework, dinner, teeth brushing, stories, kisses, excuses, and, finally, sleep, we log in again, to check e-mail and catch up on work.

As working moms, we take on multiple programs and problems, from volunteering at school and driving on field trips to running meetings and managing multi-million dollar projects. If we are lucky, we have a few hours a week to exercise, read a good book, or visit with beloved girl-friends. There is usually a sacrifice at work or at home that must be made to eke out those hours from our schedule.

If we are not careful, the physical and mental burdens that we carry every day, even though they bring us joy and satisfaction, pile up, and we find ourselves shrinking, slouching, hurting, ducking our heads, and not making eye contact with other humans.

Working moms, I am virtually smacking you between the shoulder blades! *Stand Up Straight!* Good posture is an important step in balancing the burdens of life!

Good posture makes us look and feel healthy, empowered, and in control. Standing tall makes us feel tall, and if we feel tall, we *are* tall! Straightening up and throwing back our shoulders brings about an almost instantaneous attitude adjustment and makes others perceive us as larger than life.

Good posture reduces strain on our muscles and spine, helps maximize energy and vitality, and helps prevent health issues as we age. And last, but certainly not least, another true benefit to good posture is that it makes our clothes look better and makes it more com-fortable to wear killer shoes!

I find that if I take a moment, straighten up, throw my shoulders back, and take a deep breath, the burdens feel lighter, my body feels and looks better, and my attitude is transformed. Thanks, Granny.

4 Organize the Everyday Stuff

I realized that I had to organize the everyday stuff to save time and do what I wanted and needed to do.

Suma Ramachandran is a 34-year-old writer, editor, and trainer living and working in India. She returned to full-time work two years ago, after working from home for three years. She is fortunate to have her mother take care of her son when she's at work.

I'm a very organized person at work, but I used to be just the opposite at home. I gave up working full time after my son was born. It was a conscious decision made without any regrets. When my son was about three years old, I began working from home. During this time, I somehow managed to muddle through the everyday housework.

When I went back to work, I didn't transition into the new routine very well. The full load of housework and all the shopping, in addition to nine hours or more at the office, left me dead on my feet. Worse, I wasn't spending any exclusive time with my son! Indian cooking—particularly northern Indian cooking—is labor intensive, which meant I was spending at least an hour in the kitchen every morning and another hour in the evening. So, when my five-year-old wanted me to come and see how his new toy airplane worked ("It's awesome, Mom! You have to see this"), I couldn't, because I was slaving over a stove. Just as bad was the fact that I had no "me" time.

One evening, I caught sight of myself in a mirror at a grocery store and gasped. Literally, gasped. That reflection in the mirror—an exhausted, sleep-deprived, miserable-looking, overweight woman was me? I promised myself right then and there that things would change. I needed to deploy my workplace organizational skills at home, pronto! I realized that I had to organize the everyday stuff to save time and do what I wanted and needed to do.

I started to create more detailed to-do lists and decided to plan weekly menus. On Fridays, I made a list of everything I needed for cooking the next 12 meals. On Saturday, I bought everything I needed down to the last bit of seasoning.

On Sundays, I hung up five-to-six outfits with accessories dumped in the pockets or on the clothes hanger to ease the morning rush. They're not always ironed. Yet, not having to decide, hunt, match, and coordinate an outfit saves me a lot of time. I'm still not too good at adhering to this, but I try. After all, clothes make the working mom, too!

To keep things uncluttered and orderly, we decided as a family that if we bought anything, we'd have to give something away. So, if we buy new clothes or a pair of shoes, we make sure we give away something old. Where this really works is with my son's toys. So now, when he gets a new toy, he has to pick one to give away. He got used to that pretty quickly (and it is a great lesson in generosity).

These three things helped me save, on average, around 6-8 hours a week. Now, every day, I have more time to spend with my son—whether it's watching him take an hour to set up a maze of race car tracks in his room, or bake his favorite cake together, or simply talk to him about his day. Equally important, I have time for myself. I can take a late evening walk, chat with my neighbors (without worrying about what to make for dinner), organize potluck lunches, or take a hobby class. Moreover, I still manage to get "free" time to curl up with a book or indulge in some messy finger painting with my son.

5 Take a Time Out

Sometimes, by trying to do everything, you just wear yourself down.

Andrea Vos (37) lives in Amsterdam with husband Jan Willem, son King (3) and daughter Lux (1). She is an independent interaction designer and works for several renowned agencies and clients.

As a working Mom, there is usually very little time to spend on yourself. There is always one more thing: that one last e-mail, one more load of laundry, a few more things to pick up. Sometimes, by trying to do everything, you just wear yourself down. The funny thing is, you end up not doing anything especially well; you're not a better mom or partner or boss or colleague or employee.

Try to see yourself as a totally hot sports car. You can just use any old gasoline and oil to keep the engine running on a basic level, but anyone would agree that's a waste of a perfectly good sports car. You need to take special care of the car with regular tune-ups, top-of-the-line parts, and tons of TLC to radically improve its performance and lifespan.

It may sound contradictory, but being selfish can make you a better person and help you cope with all your challenging roles. It took me quite a while to find the right balance, and I still sometimes slip into the comfortable routine of trying to do everything. I've learned that I really need to take some time off from my busy schedule and just spend it on... ME!

If it's hard for you to invest time in yourself and your sanity, try taking it slow and working your way up. Start with a quiet cup of coffee and a nice magazine, or a quick shopping trip during lunch. Anything that takes you out of the routine for an hour or so each week is good by me. You can work your way up to lunch or dinner and a movie with your friends. You can go shopping for a few hours, as long as you only buy stuff for yourself! Of course, you could include your partner in this special "you" time, if that's what you want. We regularly have a sitter over and have dinner together, just the two of us. A nice dinner and some wine—it's a real live date!

As I now consider myself quite advanced (ahem), I sometimes block time in my calendar without even knowing what I'm going to do. What a wonderful treat. It brings back some of the spontaneity you kind of lose when you have kids and a demanding job. Usually, I spend time with friends I haven't seen for a while. There's the added bonus that your friends with less hectic schedules no longer see you as ruled by the calendar, your job, or your offspring.

Find a way to fit it in. Find something that works for you, your life, and your priorities. My "me-time" has a social character. I want to see friends and really have the time to talk and enjoy their company. A lot of retail therapy also takes place in this time, just walking around town, browsing through the shops, and enjoying a long lunch with a stack of magazines.

You will get a fantastic return on your investment in yourself. You'll find you have more energy, less stress, and much more patience towards your children, partner, and colleagues.

6 Daycare Is Not a Sin

If we want to maintain what we currently have, keeping our job is our only option.

Candice Blackmore has 14 years of marketing experience and is currently the Director of Marketing for a fresh vegetable processor in central California. She is mom to a two-year-old daughter.

From the moment that little "+" appeared, I knew my life would change. Not for the cliché reasons many think when they get the same result, but for the simple fact that I work.

The decision to continue employment is complex for any family. From personal beliefs to financial ability, it is usually one of the more stressful aspects of parenting. Like countless moms before me, as soon as I became "visibly" pregnant, *that* question began to pop up: "Will you continue working?"

Growing up in my family, being a mom *was* the job and a career was somehow selfish. Today, my friends see working as part of life, like it or not. If we want to maintain what we currently have, keeping our job is our only option. For me, it simply came down to the fact that I enjoy what I do. Like others, I invested time, money, and effort to achieve what I have. With my decision to continue my career after my child was born came the inevitable (and unenviable) task of locating great child care.

I compare finding daycare to finding the right man…good appearance, well-mannered, responsible, trustworthy, clean, gentle-natured, caring and *a-hem* "affordable." As any working mom can attest, the search is part art and part science with a ton of intuition. Despite the weeks of disappointing searches through homes with dirty toys, bruised kids running in diapers, blaring televisions, bulldog populated yards (yes—pit bulls!), I *finally* found someone who clicked with my child and me.

My daughter was 4 months old at the time. I was nervous at the thought of daycare, but I looked forward to returning to work. On our big day, we headed out like excited kids on the first day of school. Many associate the term "separation anxiety" with children, but in this case, it was me. After reassurances that my daughter would be held, cared for, and fed, I finally left.

I have to admit, that first day wasn't my most productive. I had overwhelming thoughts of guilt and could hear people talking, but, like the muffled voice in a Charlie Brown cartoon, all I heard was "wohhh, wohhh, wohhh, wohhh." I must have called the provider a dozen times. Is she crying? Is she alone in some swing? Is she hungry? Tired? Each time I called, my provider politely reviewed what happened since we last spoke. Somewhat ashamed by my behavior, I thanked her for her time—again. Now, about that work...

The calls grew fewer and eventually stopped as I grew more comfortable with the arrangement. Daycare was now a normal part of our day...a time for my daughter to play, to learn, and be cared for by someone I trusted. It was also time for mommy to be productive outside the home and not feel guilty about it. My comfort with daycare is based on the fact that I trust my provider *completely.* We worked together on potty training and giving up the pacifier, adopting each other's techniques along the way. Daycare works well for us because of our *trust* and the *collaborative relationship* we have developed. More importantly (to my employer at least), this was key to keeping me focused during the day.

Part of me feels guilty that I am not the one to experience certain things with my daughter. I also know that this is a great opportunity, and I am happy when she is excited to share her day with me. I have to admit, it does take a bit of "letting go." I've decided it is a healthy way for us both to develop as individuals and as a family.

I'm a better mom because of daycare, and she is a better child. I don't regret my decision a bit. Daycare is not a sin.

7 Outsource Everything You Can

... No one can shop, clean or cook for your family as well as you can.

Hilary Glann is married with two sons and four pets. A former executive with HP, Hilary now runs a marketing consulting firm that helps technology companies use marketing as a competitive advantage.

As a working mom, time is your most precious commodity. Motherhood and career are both all-consuming activities; you don't have time to do it all yourself. Since they'll probably notice at work if you ask others to do your job for you, your only choice is to outsource some of your family chores to others.

This can be difficult for many because, after all, no one can shop, clean or cook for your family as well as you can. However, you're not Martha Stewart, who actually gets paid for being a household wizard. Instead, focus on being Mom at home and let others take care of the rest. Here are some simple ways to have others do work for you:

- **Buy online:** Many grocery stores now offer affordable home delivery. And, if you plan ahead, you can get free or inexpensive shipping on many other Internet purchases. Okay, so online shopping is not without its perils—one time Safeway delivered 12 pounds of green beans instead of 2 because I typed the order quantity wrong. But green beans aside, online shopping can save you tons of hours and shopping hassles.

- **Have someone else clean the house:** Get back the time that you're spending cleaning your house. If you can't afford or can't find someone to clean your house for you, then make house cleaning a family affair. Spend a couple of hours together, as a family, on Saturdays cleaning your home. Sure, you'll have some uneven results from the kids, but, really, who cares? The kids are learning how to be self-sufficient, the family is all working together, and you're not a bitter solo toilet scrubber.

- **Be an Excellent Carpooler:** Seek out carpool opportunities for as many of your kid's activities as you can. Sell your children on the "green" benefit of carpooling if they dislike the kids they have to carpool with. Carpools take some upfront time to organize, but can save huge amounts of time in the end.

- **Make Your Kids Part of the Solution:** Most kids "needs" vastly outnumber their means. Instead of listening to endless whining from your kids about the toys they need, have them earn these rewards by working for you. If your kids ask for specific things, work out a plan with them to take on extra chores to "pay for" those items. My son earns a subscription to a satellite soccer channel by carrying out some very specific chores each week. He can stop doing the extra chores at any time—and we'll stop paying the sub-scription fee.

Many moms are uncomfortable putting their kids to work—between school and extracurricular activities, so many kids are already over-scheduled. But, kids who help out more at home are learning about the value of money and the value of their time. Plus, they're gaining an ap-preciation for how hard their parents work to support them. These are valuable skills that will make them self-sufficient when they leave home. Any child over the age of five can contribute to the well-being of the family in some way or another.

There are many other ways to outsource work to others. It's up to your budget, and your creativity, to figure out the right balance of do versus delegate.

8 Never Give Up

I make it a rule never to give up on anything, especially myself.

Susan Guerrero, a parent and educator, has written several plays concerning women's issues and has been a contributor and editor for "Poets for Peace" and "Words of Women."

As a single working mother, I am responsible for 501 children. Four of them I gave birth to: triplet daughters and a son. By all rights, I should live in a shoe, except that, unlike the old woman who did, I know exactly what to do. As an elementary school principal and a parent, I love every child I work with as if they are my own. I never give up on learning how to serve them and the community better. In fact, I make it a rule never to give up on anything, especially myself.

Years ago, as a young married woman wanting to start a family, I was told I would never have a child. While initially my doctor was right, I ended up having triplets instead. Three months after the girls were born, I was getting a divorce and facing the reality of having no husband, no job, and no prospects. I had to go on welfare and was constantly told, "You will never amount to anything."

My choice was either to get lost in the social welfare system or to fight to redefine it. I decided not to give up. I figured that as someone who could breastfeed two babies at a time while also alternating a third, I had multi-tasking skills that could be utilized to my advantage. I also had an extended family that loved and supported me and a community that embraced my children and me as their own special project. This was important to me then and remains vital to me now. Who I am, both as a parent and a professional educator, resulted from the things I experienced. My experiences taught me that there are always choices and possible solutions, but you won't find them if you give up.

It was humiliating to be on welfare. At every turn, there were people who made sure to insult me verbally and judge me. Former friends, acquaintances, even professors at the college I attended questioned the choices I made as a parent. "Why are you leaving your children to go to class?" "Shouldn't you be working?" "Why did you bring these children to class?" "Shouldn't you be at home?" "You should quit."

On the other hand, I also met people who encouraged and assisted me, guiding me toward programs to help me stay in college and pay for it. One of these people, Pam, was an amazing woman I met through the "Mothers of Twins." Pam, an African American mother of triplets, was also on welfare. She had triplet babies almost the same age as my daughters, as well as an older child. Pam didn't have the kind of support I did from family and neighbors, yet she would not give up. Her tenacity inspired mine. Her mantra was, "I will succeed."

The day I succeeded in graduating from college, my toddler daughters stood on the hill of the stadium with a sign that read: "We're proud of our graduate mommy." It's a memory they often refer to when sharing their doubts about their own education or life choices. Education was important to me then, and so it remains the center of my life even after 20 years as an educator. Every day, I know in the deepest part of myself that women, especially mothers, must never give up on themselves in order to be there for their children. Whether our work is in our homes, our communities, or a place of business, we need to continuously develop ourselves.

This June, I will be standing with my son holding signs for my daughters, who are graduating from college. Their signs will read "Never Give Up!"

9 Find Great Partners

The only way I thought I could "do it all" was to not do it all.

Sally Thornton is president and co-founder of Flexperience, a boutique Bay Area firm that connects experienced professionals with part-time, flex-time, or project-based work.

For those working moms considering the entrepreneurial path (the word "momtrepreneur" is still a little odd to me), I suggest you find great partners. The odds of any new business succeeding are daunting, to be sure, and then adding on to that our responsibilities as moms—it can leave even the most fantastic idea unexecuted.

The rewards of creating my own path, on my own terms, inspired me to think about *how* I could do it—not *if* I could do it. The only way I thought I could "do it all" was to not do it all. Instead, I would share the excitement *and* the workload, by getting the brainpower and experience of other talented moms who shared my values and goals, while adding complementary skills. I think this is especially critical when I wondered what leader has strategic vision, financial acumen, creative juices, management skills, selling instincts, operational expertise, *and* wants to spread herself so thinly? I find talented MBA moms to be especially challenged by thinking they should do all the tasks they have learned how to do. Just because you have the capability to do something, doesn't mean you "should" do it. You might instead choose to partner and find the yin to your yang.

I knew choosing the right partners was the first and most important decision I would make in starting the company I founded in 2006. When I met my co-founder, Lara, I knew I could launch Flexperience. Lara had the skills, the passion, and the values that complemented mine. Together, we could do this almost like a "job share."

Literally, the first day I met Lara, I pitched her the business idea (she thought she was just coming for a play date for our little girls!), and we launched the company seven months later. Weeks later, my friend Michelle said she was interested in joining us, and it took only a few months to realize that we couldn't have done it without all three of us. Together, the three of us not only complemented each other professionally, but we motivated each other personally and had a lot of fun along the way—which is critical, as there are so many reasons (for example, not making any money the first year) to pull out.

The idea of partnering also applies more broadly to finding great organizations to help each other's business grow. For example, before launching Flexperience, I found a great start up called "MommyTrackd.com." I asked the founder for advice on launching, and we ended up staying in touch. I somehow was able to convince them to co-sponsor an event that we called "Mother + Professional = New Formulas for Success."

The idea was to have a panel of working moms who all took creative paths to an interesting professional role, so an audience of moms could find practical tips/tricks for negotiating part-time, flex-time, job-shares and be inspired by the fact that there is a lot of grey area between the black and white choices of working full-time or staying at home with the kids. Our partnership called for Flexperience to handle most of the work (it was our idea, after all) and for MommyTrackd.com to help us land cool panelists and sponsors.

It was fun when they thought we'd be lucky to pull a hundred people, and we had 420 attendees the first time, and a sold-out crowd of 600 the second time! Together, we achieved a lot more than either of us would have achieved alone. And...we had fun along the way.

10 Eat Meals Together

It would be so easy to sit in front of the TV and zone out while we eat, but my son and I really enjoy our dinnertime.

Jen Berkley is the proud mother of her terrific son, Matt, who is proud of keeping his Mom on her toes 24/7.

As my son enters his teen years, I hear warnings from well-meaning friends about how he'll be "checking out" and ceasing to communicate very soon. There is one staple of our home life that I'm committed to in hopes that it keeps communications open—our family mealtime.

As a single parent, it takes more effort to make a "family mealtime" happen since there are just two of us. It would be so easy to sit in front of the TV and zone out while we eat, but my son and I really enjoy our dinnertime. This is an opportunity to share the happenings of the day, debate about music, laugh at the latest celebrity gossip, plan future vacations, etc.

I grew up with this as a family ritual…as did most of my friends. "Back in the good old days," families didn't have as many different activities to pull them apart in the evening: extracurricular sports, tutoring, piano lessons, MySpace, hundreds of cable channels, text messaging, online poker, and on and on. Life was so much simpler back then (I can't believe I just wrote that!). Today, families and family time are still important. But back then, there were certain times of the evening that everyone just knew not to call another household or set their kids loose in the neighborhood.

I definitely feel as if I'm fighting the tide at times, but so far I'm winning. Even when my "man child" is in the middle of football season and doesn't get home until after 9 p.m. for dinner, I'll wait and serve a full meal. This is all instinct for me...it *feels* right...I *enjoy* this time with my son. It seems like the right thing to do. Plus, there is research that backs me up.

A study by the National Center on Addiction and Substance Abuse (CASA)[1] found that kids who eat with their families fewer than three times per week are much less likely to think their parents are proud of them and are more than twice as likely as more frequent family diners to say there is a great deal of tension in their family. Kids who eat most often with their parents are 40 percent more likely to get A's and B's in school than kids who have three or fewer family dinners per week. Children who don't eat dinner with their families are 61percent more likely to suffer from depression, and/or use alcohol, tobacco, or illegal drugs.

And for those of you with older kids, don't assume that they aren't interested in sharing the family mealtime. In the CASA study, the majority of teens who ate three or fewer meals with their parents wished they did so more often.

Some ideas for how to make family mealtime more interesting:

- Turn off the TV.
- Ask questions like, "What was your favorite part of your day?"
- Ask kids and adults to talk about a book they are reading or a movie they want to see.
- Get everyone's input to plan your next family outing or vacation.

I love this quote from Robin Fox, an anthropologist at Rutgers University: *"A meal is about civilizing children. It's about teaching them to be a member of their culture."* What a great summary of our jobs as parents...civilizing our children...teaching them to be contributing members of society. The family meal is a great tool and tradition to help battle all of the other factors in our society that make our job so challenging.

Bon appetit!

---

1. The complete CASA study can be found at http://tinyurl.com/3fgsmc

Succeed at Staying Fit

... Choose to burn extra calories all day long in small doses.

Krista Leopold has over 20 years of dance and fitness experience. She helps others succeed in achieving their wellness goals. She works full-time in web development, while teaching fitness classes in Charleston, SC.

The plight of working mothers is that as our schedules fill up, caring for our own health gets squeezed out. For working moms with little time, there is good news—you can be fit without committing to long hours in the gym. By abandoning some preconceived notions and making a few simple changes, you can succeed at staying fit.

You do not have to look like a cover model to be happy. This destructive idea is also the one that you pay hard-earned money to hear. Battle this thought by giving up the things that perpetuate these impossible standards. Without TV and magazines, you'll be free of constant negative reinforcement. Not only will you enjoy an improved outlook and positive self-image, you will also gain additional free time to play with your family.

Another idea you should reconsider is that exercise requires a lot of time. Don't miss out on valuable opportunities to be an active woman by thinking that exercise is just a one-hour-a-day thing. Instead, choose to burn extra calories all day long in small doses. Take the stairs; park in the last spot; tighten and release your abs while seated at your desk. There are infinite opportunities to infuse sedentary tasks with more activity.

Finally, remember that exercise doesn't have to be hard to be good. Intense workouts are necessary if you are training for a competition, but the average woman can experience fitness benefits simply by increasing her daily activity. You don't have to cancel your membership if you like your club and are able to find the time, but know that you have options. Why don't you break a sweat by putting on energetic music and dancing with your kids while dinner bakes?

As a busy working woman, you need to keep your energy up and your mind clear. To enjoy these benefits, evaluate your time and determine where you can insert a little extra movement. Here are some suggestions for adding activity to your day, without demanding more of your precious time:

- **Begin each day with gentle stretching or sun salutations.** Moving first thing in the morning will clear your mind and allow you to mentally prepare for the day. It might require getting up before everyone else, but think of it as a gift of sanity to you.

- **Look for opportunities to move instead of sitting still.** Try standing instead of sitting; walking on your lunch break; jogging in place while listening to voice mail or when on hold, or meeting your gal pals for yoga instead of a drink. Anything can be made active with a little creativity and boldness.

- **Let your children be your guide.** Play with them, imitate them, laugh with them. Instead of "Movie Night," teach them games you played when you were a kid or make up new ones together. Take nature walks and join them on the jungle gym. The best times you'll enjoy with your family start when someone says, "Who wants to play...?"

- **Let your kids exercise with you.** Hold your baby while doing wall sits; invest in a jogging stroller; put your toddler on your shoulders and do walking lunges or hoist her over your head a few times.

Physical fitness and the benefits that come with it require you to be physical. Start by making positive changes to your day that get you moving and smiling. Free yourself from preconceived notions about "working out," and you will find yourself more fit, creative and successful, both in your challenges at work and at home.

12 Stay Ahead of Your Schedule

Paper works everywhere and doesn't run out of batteries.

Alice de Sturler is a Dutch lawyer who teaches human rights at Virginia Tech. She lives in Blacksburg, Virginia with her husband and daughter.

If there is one thing working moms need to do, it is to manage their time. In my humble opinion, every working mom needs a good organizer to accomplish this. I know that electronic organizers are all the rage—Blackberrys and iPhones are super cool, but not always practical (at least not for this working mom). Paper works everywhere and doesn't run out of batteries. Soft cover, hard cover, ring-bound, glued spine, a week at a glance, one day per page, a month at a glance, spiral bound, electronic organizers...you name it, I have it (partly used and abandoned in a trunk in the basement!)

Ultimately, I keep coming back to my leather bound ring organizer with yearly refills. Advantage: old-fashioned with a quality cover that lasts a lifetime. Disadvantage: old-fashioned and pricy. But, you get what you pay for; mine dates back to the 1980s.

Now on to content: I like a horizontal week-at-a-glance. The month at a glace does not leave me enough room to write what an appointment is about, what to bring to a field trip, or whose birthday party it is. I chose refills that have the times and dates preprinted. A page per day makes the book too thick and will not fit in an average-sized handbag.

I once saw the loveliest organizer, but it had a day per page. It did not fit into any of my handbags, so I started carrying it around. It didn't take long and, you guessed it, I got annoyed with that. So I set out for the nearest department store and searched through all the handbags to see which could hold my lovely organizer. When I realized I was buying something I didn't need to carry something that annoyed me, I got so discouraged that I went back to the old format and size.

Now, make sure when you purchase your organizer that you think about how you will use it. If you leave it at home on the table, then any size and thickness will do. Leave it in the car? Better choose a cover that wipes clean easily and has a clasp to make sure you do not lose tickets or scraps of paper that invariably get tucked inside. Do you keep it in your handbag on a daily basis? Then a smaller, pocket size model is probably best.

To make sure I am on time for appointments, work, or classes, and still have some time for myself, I follow a few guidelines. At the beginning of each school year, all school drop-off and pick-up times are penciled in, making sure I catch all the early releases (they really mess up a working mom's schedule.) Next come the work schedules, mine and my husband's, plus all the family sports schedules.

I also have a few checks tucked in the cover. No cash at a store that accepts only the one credit card you do not have? No problem! Grab your handy organizer and pull out your emergency check.

If you write all school days in the calendar, it also becomes clear in the beginning of the year when the long weekends will be. That will give you a chance to keep an eye out on airfares to book a get-away with the family.

After all, that's why we plan and schedule...so we can work and raise a family without going completely crazy.

13 Be Present

When I'm happy, fulfilled and centered in who I am and what I value, I have everything to give.

Cara France is the President of Sage Consulting Associates. She holds her MBA from Stanford, is an abstract painter and world traveler, and is the mom of twin two-year-olds.

When I'm happy, fulfilled and centered in who I am and what I value, I have everything to give—to my family, my career, my community. That is the premise on which I live my life.

It's about quality. It's not the number of hours I spend with my two-year-old twins—it's the quality of that time. My gift is being "present" with them 100 percent. I love managing and growing my business. I love spending quality time with my husband. I love being with my children. The challenge is being fully present in each moment, truly sharing my "self" and my time.

It's about what I believe. I talk to mothers who feel torn—there isn't enough time for work or kids, and they feel like failures in both arenas. This isn't my experience or my belief. My approach is "it's possible to be fully engaged, fully expressed and joyful in all areas of my life that I value." I believe this is true, and it shows up in how I have chosen to live my life. No, it's not a fairy tale or the latest self-help affirmation. No, it's not always easy. Yes, it requires discipline, commitment, trust, and occasionally a little courage. It requires the willingness to explore who I am—the good, the bad, the ugly—and to look honestly at my deeply held beliefs and change the ones that don't support my values.

It's a journey. Early on, I found having my Blackberry meant I was always connected to the office, which made me feel better about taking care of my clients, but often it disconnected me from my kids. Then, I turned the Blackberry off for the three to four hours I was out with my kids. Next, I started blocking consistent days and times where I'm out of the office. That helped me to arrange my work schedule around my important "meetings" with my children. Then, I started enlisting people in my office to help support my choices and commitments. Today I have the support I need. All these practical steps allow me to be fully engaged and present with my kids.

It's a practice. Some days are better than others. It's about being aware. I notice when my thoughts and fears take over and try to bring myself back to the present. And I have to do it over and over and over. When I'm with the kids and I start thinking about issues at work, I take a few deep breaths and focus on this precious time with my children. When I'm present, it becomes obvious what the current moment is about and how to go into the next moment. Whether it's skipping bath time because the spontaneous music time is magical or meeting with a key employee because they feel there is something important to discuss, being present allows me to be tuned into what is needed in the moment. That's where the magic happens.

Yesterday, I spent the morning in swimming class with my twins—splashing and swimming, eating lunch together, then a quick change into "work clothes" and into the office for several meetings. Then, home for a wonderful family dinner where we say our gratitude prayer (luckily, my two-year-olds are grateful for Mommy and Daddy). We had an unexpected family drumming circle, skipped bath time because drumming seemed so important at the moment, and read books and went to sleep.

Everyone benefits. By focusing on being fully expressed and fulfilled, I'm able to be truly present and joyful, which impacts everyone I touch and everything I do. When I'm not fully present with my kids, they tend to get whiny, cranky, and act out. When I'm fully there, we connect. We have fun. We play and we laugh. With my husband and co-workers, it plays out the same way. Being present is a practice—one that for me makes all the difference!

14

Lose the Guilt

... It takes far more energy to be a guilty mom than a loving one.

Pamela Jimenez Castellanos lives in San Jose, California, with her husband, David and sons Benjamin, 2 ½ and Talyn, 1. Since 1995, she has worked in Human Resources at high-tech companies.

Any working mom not in denial experiences some degree of guilt from time to time. We're guilty for not being at home with the kids, guilty for not being better employees, guilty for serving take-out again, guilty that we don't do as much as our moms did and that our husbands do more than our dads did, (speaking of husbands, wait, that's a different rule), and guilty that our house is *just not that clean...* The list goes on and on.

I can think of at least seven other things I feel guilty about right now. But, dwelling on the negative is not the point. Instead, I urge all working moms to *lose the guilt.* If I don't, it will destroy me and take every ounce of self-worth, confidence, and patience I have. When this happens, the day goes downhill very fast, and I become a guilty, weepy, irrational wreck.

A perfect example was the day before I went back to work after my first son was born. Wanting to prove I was a fabulous mother and excellent housekeeper, I had a long list of chores to be done before our nanny arrived in the morning. Walking aimlessly from room to room in a fog, I was quite busy, but not focused, and accomplished nothing I had set out to do.

That night, sitting in the nursery by the dim nightlight, as my son slept angelically, I could see the dirty floor and dusty shelves. I was a guilty, sobbing mess. *I am a terrible mother; the nursery is dirty, for heaven's sake!* Calmly and quietly, my sweet husband gathered some cleaning supplies, and on his hands and knees, cleaned the room in the dark. And I felt so guilty.

In retrospect, I know that the guilt doesn't get me anywhere. It doesn't make me a better mother, change the past, help me, teach me, inspire me, or motivate me. Nor does it help my kids or my husband. It only destroys my confidence and satisfaction as a mother and wife.

Why should I feel guilty? I do the best I can.

I'm a good mom. I love my kids and they love me. In fact, they think I'm pretty fabulous (probably because they are still very young). I may not spend all day with them every day of the week, but "quality time," not "quantity time" has real value in my life. And, I appreciate that. Plus, while I am at work, I have the best possible childcare. So, I'm not guilty about that anymore.

My boys are my husband's children too. He gets home from work first, changes more poopy diapers than I do, and is better at getting them to sleep. I'm not guilty about that anymore either. Instead, I revel in the fact that I am blessed with a wonderful husband who is a fabulous and very hands-on father.

My mom, also a working mom, always told me that it takes more energy to be angry and hold a grudge than it does to forgive and forget. Using that principle here, it is obvious that it takes far more energy to be a guilty mom than a loving one. I do not know any working moms with energy to spare.

Life is short, and our time is limited. If we let the guilt creep in, we will miss out on the "quality time" and the best aspects of being a working mom. To be a successful *working mom*, you must do your best at work, and do your best at home. By all means, lose the guilt, or it will destroy you.

15 Love Your Appliances

I can balance and juggle, with the best of them.

Sandrine Chaumette is a married mother of four boys. She has spent most of her career in the high tech industry and has degrees from the University of California and Cornell. Currently, she works part-time for two mom-owned businesses.

Attending the Peking Acrobat Show a while back, I came away with one conclusion: I can do that! I can balance and juggle, with the best of them. I don't do my tricks on stage, nor do I use the same skills. My stage is my home. My acrobatics are balancing a part-time job outside the house with a full-time job at home as wife and mother.

My apparatuses are my appliances. They buy me time, decrease my effort, and assume some of my responsibilities. Using the technology built into my appliances is the foundation for my successful balancing and juggling act. Before starting your home "acrobatics," do the following:

- Take a look at your appliances' quick-start guides.
- Check out the control panel on the appliance.
- Identify and use buttons labeled "auto," "self," and "delay."

My appliances reduce the amount of effort I spend doing unpleasant tasks like cleaning my oven. I dreaded buying one of those noxious oven cleaners. I hated the idea of wearing safety goggles and safety gloves. Then I noticed the

"Self Clean" button on the oven. On a whim, I pressed the button before going to bed. When I got up the next day, the gunk had been reduced to a small pile of dust. I wiped the oven clean in 15 minutes. Wow! Also, I no longer rinse my dishes in the sink. I load the dirty dishes in the dishwasher and press "Rinse." The process takes nine minutes of the dishwasher's time, not mine. In addition the dishwasher uses less energy and less water than if I rinsed the dishes myself. Imagine that.

My appliances help me manage my time. Mornings at our house include breakfast, homework (my kids do homework at 7 a.m.), dishes, preschool drop off, elementary school drop off, all by 8:30 a.m. After all that, I drive to work. I buy myself time, by grinding my coffee beans, and setting the coffee maker to "auto" the night before. My coffee is ready and waiting at 7 a.m. I also use the countdown timer on the stove, washing machine, dishwasher, cell phone, and more. I use it to start a load of laundry after everyone is done bathing, run the dishwasher after it's filled. I can turn on the appliance when I remember but not have the process start until I am actually ready. All I have to do is decide how much of a delay I need and press the button. I absolutely hate driving to work and remembering that I forgot to start the dishwasher or washing machine. Using the "delay" buttons dramatically decreases this annoying source of stress.

I even delegate responsibilities to the appliances. There are certain television shows and stations I don't allow my children to watch. Instead of standing guard, I set up a list of our "favorites." That way, they are able to watch only the shows I approve. Also, my kids love a nightly bedtime story. I use books on CD when I am not available because of travel or illness. Delegating lets me take care of my kids' needs when I'm not physically with them.

To successfully work inside and outside the house, I delegate, manage my time, and reduce effort with the help of my appliances. Give it a try. Your life will be so much easier.

16 Not Everyone Can Work From Home

If you want to succeed in your career while raising a toddler, work far, far away from home.

Jen Dahlen, a wife and mom of twin boys, is a Denver-based designer/entrepreneur. She helps visually communicate brands among various industries and keeps her clients on their competitive edge.

If you want to succeed in your career while raising a toddler, work far, far away from home. All moms love their kids. Most love their jobs. When the option to work from home arises, what could sound better? That's what I once thought, anyway.

I was blessed with twin boys. I left my full-time position as a graphic designer with an advertising agency to stay home with them and start my own graphic design business. I loved my job, but it just didn't make sense to us to hand over almost my whole paycheck to day care. I should spend the time with them...right? It seemed like a great time in my life to become an entrepreneur—new babies, new beginnings. I was very optimistic.

The first nine months were smooth sailing—even with twins. I stayed home all day and got plenty of work done. I bought a laptop so I could be in whatever room they were in. I loved having no one to answer to. And, I loved the freedom to have things on my terms. Then, one day, they began to crawl.

I remember my sister-in-law saying something about, "Once they start to crawl, it's all over." At the time, I just thought she was being a pessimistic, burned-out mom. Besides, I was a mom of *twins*, which automatically made me a Super Mom.

I think I was in denial about how difficult working from home had grown to be. Around their second birthday, I realized how much things had changed. My home had become a zoo. I finally admitted that two-year-olds and working from home just don't mix, and that soon I was going to go crazy. I felt I was cheating my clients, cheating my children, and cheating my husband, and therefore cheating myself. Then, I made a huge mistake.

I introduced my two-year-olds to the Thomas the Tank Engine Web site. My plan was to be the "fun mom" that day. It was one of the most fun moments of their lives, since they worshiped the tracks Thomas rolls on. But, since that day, I could not open my laptop within fifty feet of my boys without them jumping up and down, begging for "a Thomas game." Of course, I cave in every time, because it is such an innocent, fun thing they want to do.

Now, my working-from-home hours are mostly limited to nap time and bed time. However, I have been able to brainstorm up a few activities to keep the little monkeys busy when I really need to follow-up on e-mails and calls during the day.

A bag full of magnets and a few pizza pans make a good toddler activity. And when the pizza pans become boring, pull out some sauce pots and show your little one how to stick them on the sides. And after that loses its luster, show him how to put a piece of paper behind the magnet and then use it as a drawing template. This type of activity can be tweaked all day! Just change up the materials to keep it interesting and new.

So, the moral is this: Some ages are more suitable to combine with working from home. Toddlerhood is definitely not one of these stages. But if you really want or have to do it, just remember that while your work is important, your child will be with you forever. Find time that is dedicated 100 percent to your little one. Then find time that is 100 percent dedicated to your work. If you try to do both at the same time, you will feel like a failure at both.

It's difficult to balance, but nothing a latte won't fix the next morning.

17 Make It Good Enough

I'll never forget the freedom I felt the first time I realized I could *buy* cupcakes for my son's class on his birthday, and NO ONE CARED...

Joan Bounacos has been married to George for over fifteen years. Together, they are raising three sons and so far have lived to tell the tale. Joan is a co-founder of ConsumerHelpWeb.com.

Perfection is in the eye of the beholder. Often, the beholder is the same person judging who is and who is not perfect.

You know who I mean: the mom whose house is always spotless; who wouldn't think of allowing her children to leave for school without a hot, cooked breakfast; who puts the fancy decorations on the homemade goodies she brings for her child's class party, sews her child's costumes for Halloween and the school play by hand, and always makes it look easy.

There are trade-offs for each decision we make, and attempting to out-do "Mrs. Jones" *and* be a working mother can lead to a stressed out mom, who feels like a failure. I'll never forget the freedom I felt the first time I realized I could buy cupcakes for my son's class on his birthday, and NO ONE CARED that they weren't the homemade ones I had always baked. If I had the time I would have baked, but that year I just didn't. So, I delegated the baking to the grocery store, the kids were still happy, and I didn't stress. They were "good enough."

"Ma Jones" might also require her children's chores to be done perfectly, or she would re-do the job herself. I'm enough of a realist to laugh at that expectation, so I applied the idea of "good enough" to the jobs I expected my boys to accomplish. How is a kid to learn to do it right if Mom always "fixes" things so they are "perfect?" I learned to praise my kids for the mostly made bed, the laundry that somehow ended up in the hamper, the garbage that DID get taken to the curb on the correct night. They knew the job wasn't done perfectly, but in accepting their attempts as good enough (for now), they were given an opportunity to do the best they could, get better as they grew more capable, and understand that Mom sometimes turned a blind eye when they took advantage of this rule.

Before I was a mom, I had a roommate, a single mom with two children who really showed me the meaning of "good enough." Once a week or so, she would come home and fix breakfast for dinner. Eggs, pancakes, and bacon—it was delicious and we always ate it up. She would say, "It'll keep body and soul together for another day." It was good enough; her kids were happy eating cereal and toast in the morning; and she was able to enjoy the rest of the night with her kids, not stressing about cooking a "perfect" dinner.

I saw a plaque once that read, "I could be a perfect parent if it weren't for my kids." Well, you have kids, and, contrary to your mother-in-law's opinion, they are not perfect. What's more important to you: impressing Mrs. Jones or lowering your standards just enough to be rewarded with time and energy to spend on you and your family?

My mother always said our house was clean enough to be healthy and dirty enough to be happy. One day your children will be grown and gone, your house will stay clean, your errands done (or maybe not). I know that my kids and I will remember the lesson that unless you can offer perfection, it's unreasonable to demand it in others.

The famous science fiction author Robert Heinlein gave me the motto I raised my children by, "Do not handicap your child by making his life easy." Accept attempts to do better as you would a crushed flower from your child's hand; gracefully, lovingly, and with thanks for trying! To be good enough, as a working mom, is a pretty nice thing.

Read and Be Read To

Learning to enjoy reading is not something that just "happens;" it needs to be encouraged and supported by the whole family.

Laura Hidalgo is a working mother and wife living in Northern California. She loves to dance and never finishes her daily "to-do" list.

No one has time to "do it all"—especially not us working moms. What is one of the most important bonding activities you can do with your child that is both educational and enjoyable? Reading.

We worry about instilling good habits, values and traditions in our children. Reading is one of life's best habits and has lifelong benefits. Reading *to* your children provides some quiet relaxing time during the day and encourages them to read—either by mimicking you or "reading" through memorization (depending on their age.) It is good bonding time, and instills early literacy in your children. Reading *in front* of them shows them that you value reading, and they are more likely to emulate something that they see consistently performed by their family.

Learning to enjoy reading is not something that just "happens;" it needs to be encouraged and supported by the whole family. The ability to read, and to enjoy reading, is a highly undervalued skill. Not being able to read—or not enjoying it—can cripple an individual throughout his or her life.

Rather than just trusting that it will all happen at school, make it a part of the educational experiences in your daily life. Read cereal boxes in the morning, or a shopping list at the store, or a recipe for dinner. Reading is completely portable. When you are out and about, your children can bring along their favorite books to keep them entertained, whether at their siblings' soccer practices, long car trips, etc., I find that reading a book when waiting for the doctor, especially if it is after work and my son is cranky or hungry, can be a great distraction and keep us all calm (at least until the word "shots" is mentioned).

If you don't have a large selection of books at home, try checking out your local library. I know that many of us have limited time, and adding one more thing to the day can be asking a lot. The resources that the library offers, without having to spend any more money at the bookstore, however, are definitely something that we can all appreciate. To be able to get new books every time they visit can really encourage children to read and plan out what they will read next. Most libraries offer story times and other activities for families, and librarians are great resources for suggesting books to read for your child's reading level.

In our family, we read at night before our son goes to bed. It gives us a chance to calm down at the end of the day, have a bit of quiet time for all of us to enjoy, and our son gets to have control over what we read. Unfortunately, that control sometimes means that we are reading *The Hungry Caterpillar* 10 times in a row (on the same night), but we also get to see what he is interested in. He also sees us reading—whether it is the mail, a magazine, or books when he plays in the living room in the evenings and on the weekends.

Being able to direct a child to read gives working mothers a chance to do any multitude of things working moms have to fit in without just resorting to TV as a distraction. You get the peace of mind of knowing that they are learning and enjoying themselves. Plus, it's *quiet* (for at least a few minutes).

19 Do Fun Stuff

I enjoy my children more when I give myself time to be with them and do things that we all like to do.

Lisa Plummer is a single mother of four children and one grandchild. She has degrees in Theology and Christian Leadership and is working on a Masters in Marriage and Family Therapy. She is a Medical Instructor at Western Career College.

For a single working mom, money and time are both scarce. It is easy to get so caught up in the daily essentials so that we miss the little things... if we are not careful. Yes, we are with our children all the time. But do we really *enjoy* them? Do we remember to do fun stuff?

Sure, when they were little we pointed out every new milestone and marked it in the baby books. We called our mom or mother-in-law to let them know what new and amazing feat they had accomplished. What about now, when they are older? Sometimes it feels like all of our interactions are instructions, directions and reminders (with the exception of the required, "How was school today?" to which most kids say "Fine." End of discussion.) I've found that I enjoy my children more when I give myself time to be with them and do things that we all like to do.

Any holiday is a great excuse to get creative and spend time doing things that are just a little bit out of the ordinary. My oldest daughter, now a mother herself, has great memories of spending time with me preparing goodies for her classmates. My son, who is nine years old, still likes to take treats to his class. You can stuff goody bags with inexpensive treats like holiday-themed pencils, erasers, stickers and candy from your local Dollar Store. Purchase plain sack lunch bags and let your kids be creative and decorate the bags. Baking goodies is a wonderful activity to enjoy with your children. Make cupcakes, cookies and even ornaments (not only for Christmas) and pick colors that fit the holiday and allow your children do the frosting and decorating.

In our family, one of our favorite fun things is movie night. Ours is always on Friday, and the kids and I really look forward to this time together. They get to pick the movie and our dinner. We call it our "munchie" dinner and it can be anything...homemade chicken strips, taquitos, pizza or nachos. Of course, we always have popcorn!

Although we may not always be able to afford to take vacations with our children, we can still afford weekend get-aways. A simple camping trip, even as close as an hour drive from your home, is a fun, affordable and wonderful way for you to unwind and relax from a busy week. The kids can run, yell, swim, climb trees and get dirty (not much better than that if you're a nine-year-old boy.) It is wonderful to be able to watch them enjoy themselves with a sense of freedom they don't always have at home. Invite some friends to join you, and it's a portable party.

Tradition is a word that is overused but cannot be over emphasized. All of these activities are great opportunities to create tradition in a world that seems to be losing touch with traditions. These special family times we spend together give my kids (and me) something to look forward to and plan on.

The years with our children go by so quickly. I'm not only talking about the years when they are small. Remind yourself what great kids they are. Spend time doing creative things, make up games, go camping. We only have them for a little while.... so remember to do fun stuff.

Take Time For Now

... Nobody has fun when they're trying to have an "experience."

Carolyn Pleasance is a 38-year-old first-time mom with a two-year-old, two part-time jobs and the best husband she could ever ask for. They have two cars, one cat, and a house that looks like the Little Tykes factory.

When I was a child, I started a list of "Things I'd never do when I had kids of my own." My mom used to laugh as I added yet another item (normally right after a bout of righteous indignation over what I wasn't allowed to do).

I've remembered most of what was on my list, and my son, who's two, has benefited from the careful consideration of my childhood, since it's shaping his. I know that there's a time and place to stay up a little later, that it is okay to jump in a puddle, and that you can stand in front of the TV and not go blind. I also know that car seats are non-negotiable and that love means sometimes having to say "no." Little did I know that I'd let a big "no" slip by, one I'd never realized existed.

My dad is an avid photographer. I have memories (and photos) of myself, posed at this monument, this flower clock, animal or body of water. Sometimes I'm scowling, sometimes smiling, always standing by the "thing" we've come to see. We visited a lot of great places, saw a lot of wonderful things.

Fast forward to my son's firsts: trip to the zoo, trip to the park. There's mommy, taking a million photos, trying to get him to pose with this animal, that monument. There's my little boy, scowling, trying to escape to run, play, explore. He wants to experience the world; it's ALL the "first time" for him. I'm trying to make him have an "Experience," and he just wants to chase the sun across the sky.

We went to a small local zoo when he was about a year and a half old. He'd never seen a camel, a tiger, or a bear. There I stood, next to the enclosure, camera at the ready, waiting for the moment he'd see his first live wild animal. What did my little guy do? Ran past the animals and jumped right into the little climbing car in the playground! His idea of an "experience" was to enjoy what he knew was fun—playing, running, saying words that he'd learned (car, rock, dirt). He wasn't there to see the camels.

I was recreating my childhood, the need to make sure he had an "experience" when we went places. It's too much pressure; nobody has fun when they're trying to have an "experience." The preconceived notion of what he'd get out of it was the one thing I'd forgotten to add to my list of "no's."

My list now includes the rule: let him see things the way *he* wants to see them. When I try and "cram" experiences into his life so we can have "quality time" it actually keeps him from having the *real* experiences every child should: a mom who's there, playing with him on the jungle-gym, being in the moment, taking time for now.

I know that my mom and dad wanted to ensure that I had a childhood full of travel and family fun, and they did it, while both working full time. As a working mom, I want my son to have the same fun with me, but on his terms. I can't promise not to take a million photos though, that's one *great* thing I learned from my dad.

Mind Their Manners

The time to teach manners is not when you are sitting in the restaurant.

Hollee J. Chadwick, a former newspaper editor, works from home as a journalist, humor columnist, and book editor. She successfully raised three daughters who went on to live normal lives.

We've all experienced it. You're seated in a booth at a nice restaurant. You're enjoying your dinner, chatting amiably and quietly. Then it happens. *Thump! Splat! Mo-om! Ouch!* The kid seated in the booth behind you is banging his head against the seat back. His sister seated across from him flings butter at him, and then the back and forth accusations and kicking starts.

Right then and there you say to yourself, "My children will never act like that in a restaurant." Yeah. Right.

I was brought up in a home where courtesy was king. As far back as I can remember, I was taught to sit up straight, to chew with my mouth closed, not to interrupt the adults, and to say "Please," "Thank you" and "Excuse me."

What I learned as a new mother taking her two toddlers to a restaurant for the first time was: *Be Prepared.* The time to teach manners is not when you are sitting in the restaurant—it's months before in the privacy of your own semi-sound-proof and spill-proof home.

I can remember my father saying over and over, "You should treat your family better than you do friends and strangers." At age seven, thinking I was taking my father's advice, I said "Good riddance" to two of my childhood friends as they left our backyard to return home. When my dad, who was standing nearby raking leaves, corrected me, I quickly ran, mortified, after my friends and explained that I thought "Good riddance" meant the same as "Goodbye." Thankfully, they were also seven years old, so they had no clue I had insulted them.

Teaching your child to chew with his mouth closed and to use a fork or spoon may be a lesson in patience for you. Especially, if your little angel has been allowed to "break the rules" here and there (like spitting or throwing food, eating with those sticky little fingers, or playing finger paints with pudding while you aren't looking.)

We make our own mountains out of molehills. We laugh at how cute baby Jane is being when she spews the peas across the table, reinforcing this feat with our positive reaction. Who doesn't love watching baby Johnny dig his hands and face into the cake on his first birthday? What's cute for a baby isn't acceptable for a five-year-old, or a 12-year-old, for that matter.

Punishment is not necessary when the wee tyke does this, but neither is positive reinforcement. Once may be cute, but after that it wears on you and makes your job harder, especially since raising your child is not your *only* job. Take it from a mother who has worn oatmeal to work on a wool suit because I didn't have time to change clothes after my precious decided to play show and spit. Back in the '80's, I went to work once with a chunk of scrambled egg in my hair. Those were the *big hair* days, too. Yuck.

There is nothing harmful to your children in insisting they sit properly at the table and not wander around, eating whenever they please. If they would rather wander around, then they are not hungry. Simply removing their plates to the kitchen worked wonders for me. Meals are meant to be enjoyed by all parties, not just by the children.

Manners are not a punishment, nor are they tedious. Manners make everyone more comfortable and keep things running smoothly. They make it possible for other people to enjoy the presence of your children as much as you do.

22 Separate the "Anxiety" from "Separation Anxiety"

Distract kids from any negatives and re-focus them on the fun, positive aspects of the situation.

Jennifer Blaney is the General Manager for ITEX Corporation, based in Bellevue, Washington. She has a B.S. in Business Administration from the University of Phoenix, and calls Snoqualmie, Washington, home.

We moved to a new house this year, which meant moving our four-year-old son, Alexander, to a new preschool. Alex was so enthusiastic about the move that for weeks before, he kept telling everyone that "today" was his "last day." When the big day did come, and we walked into the new school, Alex immediately took to exploring the room. He barely gave me a kiss goodbye, and one of the teachers remarked on how smoothly that had gone.

I felt rather smug about the whole deal. Reality set in when I picked him up that afternoon. Alex burst into tears as soon as he saw me. The teacher explained that although he had done "fine," he cried quite a bit. I asked Alex why he was sad. He only said, "I don't like school." So much for smug.

Each morning after that, Alex cried and clung to me. I tried to stay with him a little longer, engaging him in a book or a game until I could "slip away." There was no slipping away. Each morning, I would have to pry his fingers off my coat or hand, desperately scanning the room for an adult who would help me. I would leave in tears myself, wondering if I had made a terrible mistake in choosing the school. The final straw came one morning when a teacher offered the following advice, "You should try to leave more quickly." My incredulous reply to that was, "Yes! Let's do that! Now, help me do that."

It took two full weeks of traumatic mornings before Alex finally stopped crying, though it seemed much longer. It has taken me months to figure out what I did wrong. In the end, I know I didn't do anything wrong. It took many small, subtle tricks to make Alex less anxious about pre-school, and turn him into someone who looks forward to it. If only I had learned these tricks earlier! The key for us was distraction.

Distract kids from any negatives and re-focus them on the fun, positive aspects of the situation. Call it "school" instead of "daycare" to set the expectation that they go there to learn, that they are becoming a big kid, and they will begin to associate school with fun activities. Begin distracting even before they get to school. Keep them occupied in the car on the way. I let Alex bring his small backpack, full of toys, in the car with him every day. He plays with them on the car ride in, and we chat, giving him little time to worry about being away from home or anything else about school that may cause anxiety.

I initiated a little ritual by talking about which of his toys wave back at him while he is waving goodbye to me out the window of the school. Out of the toys in his backpack, Alex can request one of them to wave goodbye to, instead of having to say goodbye to me. Sometimes I surprise him by holding up a different "friend" to wave. In his curiosity to see who will wave goodbye to him, Alex forgets to be anxious about the day. I can get in and out in less than five minutes each morning.

Adjusting to a big change, like attending daycare for the first time or changing schools, can be traumatic for everyone involved. Remember that you can take the anxiety out of separation anxiety by distracting your children from the negative and re-focus them on the positive. I know it's possible to minimize the drama and turn you kid into one who enjoys his days. I know, because yesterday morning, as we decided that Alex was too sick to go to school, my son broke out into tears... because he didn't want to miss a single day.

I'm back to being smug!

23 Have Sex

There are all kinds of sex in a marriage.

Holly Garcia, mother of four, has been happily married for 22 years to her high school sweetheart. She works full time in the high tech industry.

Have Sex! Make Love! Cuddle! Do all of the above! Look...men and women are, shall we say, different. Keeping your partner happy contributes to your happiness, which, in turn, contributes to the attitudes and mood you share with your children. A happy attitude goes a long, long way when it comes to raising happy kids.

Haven't you noticed that when you and your partner are distant or have argued over something trivial, that even that gap in closeness impacts your mood, patience and the amount of joy you find you have with your kids? Humans need sex. It is a key way for us to feel close, loved and, yes, less stressed. Less stress means more happiness and a better attitude about all kinds of things.

There are all kinds of sex in a marriage. For my husband and me, it runs the gamut from sleepy "roll-over" sex to making love and connecting at a level that surprises us even after 22 years of marriage. Each of those kinds of sex has its merits. I know, sometimes you're too tired, either physically or emotionally, because of all of the demands on your day. From work, to kids, to house, to other obligations, by the time you pour yourself into bed, you really aren't in the mood to put much energy into anything else but sleep.

I understand, but let's get real. Sometimes, a tiny bit of energy goes a long, long way. That when it's time for sleepy sex. With minimal effort, you can manage to take care of the physical need to connect. It won't be perfect sex. It won't be movie sex. It won't really be "love making." But, it does serve its purpose.

Acknowledging the different types of sex and the importance they play in any relationship was an important lesson for me to learn. Early on in our marriage, I thought that every time we had sex it had to be perfect, deserving of our full attention, a real love-making session. Those times are magical. But what happens if you don't always have the energy for that kind of sex? Someone ends up disappointed. That can lead to a lot of subtle and not-so-subtle stress. Communication becomes strained and negative. That negativity impacts your mood and attitude. Attitude is nearly everything when it comes to having a healthy marriage and raising happy children. It's not worth trying to have perfect sex all the time. Plain old sex does the trick most of the time.

My mother-in-law, of all people, reinforced this idea with me. I don't even recall the conversation, and today I can't image the context under which the topic of sex could have possibly come up between my mother-in-law and me. I recall the big take-away from what must have been our subtle conversation on this topic. In general, she managed to get across to me what I'm trying to get across to you, although she was much more subtle and clever. The message is this—sex doesn't have to be perfect to have the desired effect. Sex makes us happy, lowers stress, and keeps us connected. Even if it isn't our perfect preconceived notion of what sex is supposed to be, it can still be pretty good.

Again, there are all kinds of sex. Enjoy them all, even the kind where there appears to be nothing in it for you, at least, at the time. In the end, you'll find that everyone is happier, life is good, stress is low, attitudes are positive. It's as simple as that.

24 Plan a Power Lunch

Not everyone will understand what it takes to be Superwoman.

Christina Johnson Polk is mom to Max, two, and wife to Kevin. She lives in Lafayette, CA, and works full time as a construction manager.

Forget taking that all-important client to the newest bistro to schmooze and impress—the idea of a "power lunch" takes on a whole new meaning for working moms. You've got a lot to do to balance your career, your household, and your personal time. So, get creative with your lunch hour and use the time to tackle things that take time away from your family and friends after work.

Can't find time to exercise? Find a gym within walking distance of the office (or with easy parking). Walk around the block or find an enjoyable destination like an inner-city park or a hillside with a view. I know you might be thinking "easier said-than-done," but try it. I've been happily surprised by how refreshing it is to get out of the office and get some exercise.

If you are socially inclined like I am, invite your co-workers (like other working moms). If you want more privacy and "alone time" take your "lunch" a little earlier or later than normal. If you don't want to sweat (or have a "bad hair day") do some weight-lifting, thoughtful meditation, or a few relaxing yoga poses.

Do you feel disconnected from your girlfriends? Schedule a gossip session. Send out an Outlook appointment with a free conference call-in number to your social circle. When several women in my Mom's club went back to work, we really missed each other and hearing about all the kids. Now we call in once a month to reconnect and hear what's up with our clamoring toddlers.

You can catch up with family, too; call your sister in Cleveland or your dad in Detroit. If you work in cubicle-land and are self-conscious about your conversations, reserve a rarely used conference room or take your cell phone for a walk (and kill two birds with one stone).

Errands taking up your weekend? Get them out of the way during lunch. Hit the grocery store to pick up a sandwich and get your shopping done, too. Keep a cooler in the car for cold stuff so it will keep through the afternoon. Find a dry cleaner close to work so you can easily fit this activity into your day instead of on the way home. Go to the local toy store (and support local businesses) and stock up on kids' birthday gifts. You won't have to make a late night trip to the "big box" toy store for your son's best friend's birthday party that you just remembered the night before.

Can't remember the last time you did something for yourself? Take some time to re-group, refresh, and relax. Head out to a local cafe with a trashy magazine. Find a discreet salon and get a pedicure—skip the polish if you get anxious about getting back to work.

Whatever you do, don't feel guilty about using this time to get your stuff done. There are times when we need to use our lunch hour to catch up on all our job-related action items. There are other times when we need to use this time to catch up on our personal action items.

You might need to be discreet if your work environment suffers from an overzealous work ethic. Not everyone will understand what it takes to be Superwoman. We need every minute of every day, so make lunch your power hour.

25

B Sur Ur Kds No U Hav a Lif

(Translation: Be Sure Your Kids Know You Have a Life!)

... Our children need to understand that we do, indeed, have lives outside of them.

Molly Wendland juggles work and family in Kansas City with her two teenage daughters and her Big Strong Man (a.k.a "Rock"). Molly writes a blog called "Balancing Act" for Disney's Family.com.

You're thinking to yourself, "My kids know I have a life. I work. I pay the bills. I keep them in juice boxes (or Juicy Couture, depending on the age group)." Nope. Chances are, they do not know. Trust me. I have a job. I write two different blogs, and I am a contributing author to two books. I have another home-based business. Plus, I belong to a fabulous book club and numerous other organizations. I, too, thought my kids knew I had a life outside of them and their self-centered, teenage planets. But then, one day, the reality came crashing down on me. They didn't have a clue.

I had confiscated my teenage daughter's phone and was skimming through her texts to see just how many she had sent during "forbidden" hours when I came across this one, referencing my ability to drive her on a future outing with friends: **"Dnt wory my mom cn driv trst me she has no socl lif"** (Translation: Don't worry, my mom can drive. Trust me, she has no social life.)

There it was. My life, summed up in 50 characters or less. My very existence, in fact, had been reduced to that of *Taxi Driver*. Never mind the consequences of my 13-year-old's actions; that's another story altogether. The point is that our children need to understand that we do, indeed, have lives outside of them.

I don't need them to praise my achievements or hail my efforts regularly. I am a self-confident woman who can handle her own in a board room or a nursery, thank you very much. However, I do expect them to recognize the sacrifices that I make for them on a regular basis. Yes, I am their mother. Yes, I signed on for this when I donated the egg. Now it's up to me to ensure that they grow up to respect their elders and not take on the sense of entitlement that so many of our young people today seem to possess.

Here are some tips to make certain that your child is aware that you have a life outside of their little universe:

- **Don't automatically say "yes."** When she asks to have a friend over, don't automatically say yes. Take a moment to physically check your calendar. If you have a conflict, do not re-arrange it unless the play date is of *supreme* importance to your child.

- **Take them to work.** Take your child(ren) to "Take Our Daughters and Sons to Work Day." This program helps illustrate the value of a balanced work and family life and normally takes place in April. Your children will learn a little about what you do all day and, perhaps, they'll come away with a greater understanding with what it means to be a working mom. For more information, you can visit their website at: http://www.daughtersandsonstowork.org.

- **Let them make their own dinner.** Once a week or so, have an evening when the kids are on their own for dinner. A friend of mine refers to this as "Yo-Yo Night." Delivered with her thick southern drawl, it was originally "Yo Ahwn Yo Ohwwn!" Everyone fends for themselves, which could mean anything from cereal, to frozen entrees, to leftovers, to the kids coming up with their own masterpiece. You get the idea.

When my daughter got her phone back, she received this text:
"Sory cnt drv u n e wher n e tim soon i hav a lif luv mom"
(Translation: Sorry, can't drive you anywhere anytime soon. I have a life. Love, Mom)

Focus

I love how my roles as a mother and as a professional stretch me in new directions and inspire me in different ways.

Shea Fialdini lives in Seattle with her husband and three children. She works as the Grants Manager for the Global Health Program at the Bill & Melinda Gates Foundation.

As a working mom, I thought I was beginning to master the fine art of productive multi-tasking, until my three-year-old son set me straight.

One day, I was trying to do too many things at one time, including getting him a bowl of ice cream for dessert. Apparently, it wasn't working for him. He looked directly into my face and said, "focus!" I laughed it off at the time, thinking it was just a cute comment, but I found myself hearing that little voice in my head over and over again, especially when I was trying to do too much.

Like everyone, I play a lot of roles in my life; I'm a wife, mother, daughter, manager, professional, sister, friend, etc. These roles all come with responsibilities and demands that make it challenging to pay attention to what's in front of me at any given moment.

As I go to work each day and come home again, I find the transition from my role as a mother to working professional and back to a mother again to be particularly humbling and humorous at the same time. The stark contrast between these two parts of my life can make me feel a little nutty sometimes.

It never ceases to amaze me that within the span of two hours I can go from having a conversation with my son about why he can pee standing up but he can't try to poop the same way, to sitting in a conference room with three other people discussing the finer points of financial risk management in international grant making. Both conversations are critically important in their own right, but the contrast is so jarring that it's enough to give me whiplash.

I love how my roles as a mother and as a professional stretch me in new directions and inspire me in different ways. I find this time in my life to be both profoundly challenging and deeply rewarding.

My ability to balance the vastly different demands of being a working mom greatly depends on my capacity to be fully present and "in the moment." This means leaving the Blackberry in the car when I'm at home (or at least not reaching for it until the kids are in bed) and not worrying about how much laundry I have to do, or what I'm going to cook for dinner when I'm in a meeting.

The happiness of my family, success of my career, and mental stability are all highly dependent on my ability to give my full attention to the person or project that's in front of me. So, when I find myself thinking about my grocery list in the middle of a staff meeting or worrying about a presentation during dinner with my family, I try to remember that little voice saying "focus."

27 Cut Out the Curfew

Oh my, could it be this easy? Yes!

Shawna Todd is the happily-married mother of two children who has learned to fill her plate daily and eat through it by 11 p.m. each night.

Believe it or not, negotiating weekend curfew times for your teen driver doesn't have to be a battle.

How does one go about setting a reasonable curfew time for their newly-licensed 16-year-old high school student? Addressing this issue can be a daunting task and most likely a dilemma that faces every household.

If you thought you lost sleep when they were a newborn, think again. Those tiny worry lines all of a sudden become much more deeply etched in your face as you watch them put the car in reverse and jet out the driveway. After trying several approaches, we found the following solution to setting a reasonable curfew time.

As we all know, children will push the limit and want to stay out much longer than their parents can keep their eyes open. When our son first started to drive, we found ourselves constantly trying to negotiate with him on Friday and Saturday nights. In the beginning, we were the time initiators, giving him the expected time to return home. We made it very clear that whatever time we set, he was expected to be in the door and on his way to bed, not driving in and parking the car. He was pretty good at staying within his parameters, and if he was going to be a few minutes late, he knew that a phone call at any time of the night was appreciated.

This approach worked for awhile, but as his social calendar grew, he wanted stay out later. Each week, he would try to get us to lengthen the time; occasionally, we did, but it was a constant discussion, and it was growing old fast. Truly, it was a war over extra minutes, and the battle of the clock reared its ugly head every single weekend. We found ourselves groaning, he was complaining, and all were getting tired of the negotiations. Something had to change!

By pure chance, our 13-year-old daughter was taking a conflict resolution training course at about the time we were running out of ideas for our daunting curfew dilemma. As we sifted through the paperwork she brought home, the wheels started turning, the light bulb came on, and our answer to this whole curfew mess was right there. Hallelujah!

Answer their question with a question. Right from the very beginning, this approach worked. We can now say that "from experience" when either of our children asks, "What time do you want me home?" We found it best not to give a time, but instead answer them back with a question. "What time would you like to come home?"

More times than not, they always gave a time that was earlier than we were thinking. Even from our seasoned son with whom we had struggled in the beginning. Oh my, could it be this easy? *Yes!*

This approach gave them a feeling of control and setting their own rules. The big plus: They were always timely. Occasionally, we would extend the time by 30 minutes as a reward as long as it was reasonable. We never allowed a time after 12:15 a.m. Why the 15 extra minutes? That way, they could leave their event at midnight, not feel like the first one leaving, and have the time needed to drive home.

Now, in the process of surviving our second teen driver, we can honestly say we do not think either ever caught on to our reverse psychology.

Dare to Compare

They were the poster moms for "having it all."

Tia Yates is a Legal Assistant in house for Washington Mutual Bank, the loving wife to William and a grateful Mom to four active boys ages 2-14.

Comparison is comfortable. We compare prices and nutrition labels at the grocery store. I certainly compared my babies to my friends': percentiles, sleeping habits, first words and steps. It was not a far slide into comparing myself to other moms—unfortunately with an obscured view.

I watched these "all together" women with an amazing talent for keeping it all running smoothly. Never missing the PTA meeting, always able to manage their work schedules around the school events, and making adorable snacks. They were the poster moms for "having it all." I, on the other hand, felt as if I was always running late, taking every shortcut I could find, and collapsing into bed at night. I didn't realize it, but comparing myself to those moms was driving how I was living. It made me very critical of myself and, in turn, my family.

I had always shied away from sharing too much with moms at school or other activities. I didn't want them to see that I occasionally dropped the ball in my juggling act. It was bad enough that I felt judged by the stay at home moms. I was horrified when I would forget until the last minute that it was our week to bring snack, and I had to *buy* something from the *store!* They would *never* serve a store-bought snack! My husband would tell me I was being ir-rational, but I could not help it. I was so thankful when our school district mandated store-bought items for school.

When my third son came along, our lives changed a little more than we expected. Eventually, he would officially be labeled "developmentally delayed," but the path it took to get there, filled with specialists, and therapy appointments, sleepless nights and heavy-hearted days made me stop comparing myself to other moms. Not because I had an epiphany. I wish. It was because I did not have the energy.

I also got to know a lot of my "pedestal" moms better. They would ask how therapy was going, or if we had attained this or that goal, and suddenly their guards were down. I learned that they had their mom at home to help keep house or bake cupcakes for them, or a part-time job out of their house that allowed for more flexibility in schedule.

As things settled into life as we know it today, I realized how much more I enjoyed working the book fairs and attending the fund-raising events for the kids' schools or sports. I don't kick myself if it does not all work out perfectly, and I am not able to make every single event. I love the contributions I do make because I am doing it for myself and my children now, and not because I am trying to be like someone else, or because I will feel as if I am less of a mom if sometimes I can't swing it.

Today I love that I can accept myself as a good mom, and while I still catch myself comparing my birthday party planning skills to another mom's (I did once make a piñata from scratch, and I won't be doing *that* again), I don't let it dictate what I do, or how I feel about myself or my family.

Last week, a friend in our moms' group compared herself to me. I was taken aback because I had never imagined anyone doing that. I was happy to have the opportunity to share with her that I have a Mom who helps me shuttle kids around and a babysitter who will pull out all the stops for me.

At the end of the day, we all have different energy levels, priorities, talents, and the biggest differential of all—we all have different children. Next time you feel the urge to critically compare yourself to another mom, think of three things you are great at...and remember you fit your family perfectly.

29 Don't Let Yourself Go

I came dangerously close to becoming the "weird pajama lady."

Tina DeMattia, is 36 years old and has one child. She just earned her Marriage and Family Therapy license after completing 3000 hours of internship and two written licensing exams.

During my pregnancy, I was finishing up an internship, and working a private practice to become a psychotherapist. I had supervision twice a week, group therapy and individual therapy once a week. Needless to say, I had a lot of emotional support! I took great pride in my clothes and make-up and got my hair and nails done on a regular basis. While I have struggled with my weight my whole life, I have always tried to look as good as I could at any weight. I loved being pregnant because I didn't have to hide.

After I had my son, I was overwhelmed with how I felt about him, how inadequate I felt as a mother and how disgusting I thought I looked. I went into survival mode, and I didn't care about my appearance anymore. I came dangerously close to becoming the "weird pajama lady." I felt depressed and isolated. If I showered and ate every day it was a miracle. We ate take-out almost every night, and I didn't wear anything without an elastic waistband. All of my attention was on my baby and how to take care of him.

To be honest, I actually loved the idea of staying in my jammies all day, shuffling around in my slippers doing the "coffee fuckaround" endlessly. This goes by many names, but basically it is when you have your first cup of coffee at 8 a.m., next thing you know, it is 1 p.m. You've drained the coffee pot, you haven't showered or done anything in particular. You swear the clock is wrong; it is almost like a time warp. There was a point when I realized I had let myself go—emotionally and physically.

My regular emotional support system was gone, along with my hygiene. My TV addiction had peaked to a new high. I was obsessed with TLC's "Baby Story" and two different make-over shows. I was astounded by how many makeovers were dedicated to helping working moms get their groove back. I thought to myself, oh my God, those poor women. What happened to them that they forgot about them- selves? Then, I caught the expression on the mailman's face when I greeted him with yet another tardy bill to go out. "What's his problem?" I thought. I went inside. It was 2 p.m., I hadn't brushed my hair, I was wearing my glasses, Christmas pajama bottoms (in June,) with a stained sweatshirt and slippers. "Oh, I am one of those women now" (And I have to go back to work next week!).

I called other working mothers for advice. Most of them said, "I don't have time for that; besides, who would watch my children?" I went back to my therapy group and asked my friends for support and help. I felt guilty, at first, but then I asked my husband to watch OUR child so I could go shopping and get my hair and nails done. At that point, it did not feel frivolous to me, it was necessary. After I had completed my own makeover, I felt so much better about myself. I vowed never to let myself go ever again.

When I went back to work, I felt more confident again, and I was grateful for a reason to shower, put myself together, and activate a different part of my brain. I remember that my nanny complimented the fact that I always put myself together. She mentioned that the other mothers she worked for run out of the house wearing whatever, with wet hair, no make-up and coffee. I thanked her and smiled to myself.

It feels important to me to help other mothers realize that taking care of yourself is just as important as taking care of others. What we wear and what we look like says a lot about who we think we are and how we are doing. I encourage all working mothers to ask for help, eat right, exercise, *sleep*, get massages, get your hair and nails done, and spend some money on some clothes that fit and make you feel good. *You are worth it!*

30 Put on Your Oxygen Mask First

No way, I need to take care of my kids (husband, mother, best friend, stranger in the seat next to me...)

Victoria Ryan knows that the most valuable contribution she has made to the U.S. workplace is her ability to influence senior leaders to allow flexible time, job-sharing, part-time work, comp-time and remote employment. Today, two of five children are at home.

Have you been on a plane with your kids and heard the flight attendant tell you to put on your oxygen mask first? The immediate response is, "No way, I need to take care of my kids (husband, mother, best friend, stranger in the seat next to me...). The idea is contrary to instinct.

What does it really mean? Simply this: If you don't don your mask first, you won't be there for all those other people when they need you. For those of us with daughters, who might become working moms, too, what better opportunity to be a role model whose values are clear: I take care of me!

The question becomes, what is your oxygen mask? For each of us, the answer is different. It might be:

- Taking that hot bath when there is so much to be done outside of the bathroom.
- Going for a walk with a friend late at night when your teenager is suffering with a paper that could have been started a week earlier.
- Taking the last piece of homemade apple pie that you made and haven't yet had a piece of.

Take the mask first! Soak in the bath. Enjoy the walk. Eat the pie. Taking good care of yourself is not selfish. Au contraire, it is the most valuable gift you can give to yourself and to all who depend on you.

My "taking care of me" things are neither complicated nor time-consuming. They include:

- Physical fitness every day: a run, a walk, yoga, stretching, tennis.
- Eating well: that means healthy and the not-so-healthy on occasion, keeping the splurges special.
- Creating "alone time" for me (send the kids grocery shopping—that's a double win—the grocery shopping is done by someone other than me and I get alone time!).

When you first start taking care of yourself, you might hear some snotty, unsupportive remarks. As I was heading out for a much-needed mental health walk one night, one of my teens with a looming deadline said indignantly and with a full-blown glare, "I can't believe you are leaving right now." I came so close to canceling, but walk I did. And, guess what? She handled the "crisis" and was better because of it. I saw and heard the confidence in her. That only happened because I walked away.

Another time, I had arranged for my then-husband to take the kids on an overnight to a local hotel with a pool to get some time in the house by myself. What a treat, right? Wrong. The whining was relentless, and I nearly broke down and cancelled. I don't know where the strength came from, but I held firm as they spewed things like, "You don't love us" and (from my husband) "What will you do with all that time?" Amazingly, he lived to see morning.

Remember, if this is new behavior for you, loved ones are not used to seeing you taking good care of yourself. Stay the course. Grab that mask and breathe. Then, help them find theirs.

Volunteer Your Way

Pick one or two volunteer activities that put you in total control.

Jan McDaniel has spent the last 25 years working in various senior management positions at some of the world's largest high technology companies. She did this while raising two daughters.

It's important to be involved with your children's activities: school, church, dance, drama or sports. You don't want to be the only parent who meets the teacher for the first time at back-to-school night or open house. You want to make a positive impression with the important people that influence your children. You want to be able to have an open dialog at any time with these influencers, as well as with your children. The trick is to do it on your terms, in a way that works for you and your family.

Any of you, who have anxiously shown up for a PTA meeting or a fundraising committee, know that your time and talent is too valuable for what can often be unfocused gab fests. Take charge. Pick one or two volunteer activities that put you in total control. For instance, sign up to be room parent for your child's class. This job typically involves your assigning parents to stuff folders on Fridays or bring cookies to the mother's tea. It's the one job that puts you in the driver's seat and also allows you to work around your schedule. You can choose the fun things you want to do and assign the chores to others.

Show up early for the first open house and pounce on the field trip lists. Have your calendar ready and sign up for the first and last field trips of the year. You'll be able to schedule these trips into your calendar, meet all the kids at the beginning of the year and make a great connection with the teacher. The end-of-the-year trip is always the most fun and relaxed and typically has nothing to do with the curriculum. That is purely a selfish selection that my kids and I always looked forward to.

Take the initiative. If your kids play sports that require snacks after the games, show up for the first parent meeting with a snack schedule ready to hand out to all the parents. I've yet to meet a coach who doesn't appreciate this job being handled before it gets assigned. Put your name on the snack list for the first game, so your job is already done. That way, the coach doesn't assign you to something like volunteering on picture day (that requires you to stay all day on Saturday with a 1,000 players) or to make a banner, or worse yet, to plan the end of the year party (that requires you to collect money for coaches' gifts and to figure out who wants what on a pizza order).

At church, meet with the youth directors or head of Sunday school and explain that your tight schedule doesn't allow a long-term volunteer commitment, but you would like to do a few things throughout the year. After all, you aren't a total deadbeat, just a working mom who knows how to allocate her time. Provide an extra set of hands for a Sunday project, call parents, or, better yet, do the snack list. Anything that shows your interest and can be done at night or introduces you to the children is great. Driving to events is often fun and gives you that chance to observe the dynamics of the group your children hang out with.

Some of the best discussions with my kids are the result of my being involved in their lives. A lot of working moms feel like they don't have the time to volunteer. I've found that I can do it, as long as I do it my way.

32 Live One Life

Do you really need two lives?

Christine Kittinger loves boys Will and Joey and husband Steve—a fantastic dad who can fix anything. She is Vice President of a human resources consulting firm, Assets Unlimited.

Popular opinion in the area of work-life balance seems to hold that the best way to excel at work and at home is to keep the two lives separate. Focus only on work at work and only on the family at home. Do you really need two lives? Not me. One is quite enough, thank you!

My boys and my work are sources of great joy (more often than not) and fulfillment in my life. Over the years, I have found that incorporating my home and work lives have brought me greater happiness and success.

Enter my office, and you see photos of my boys gracing the bookcase, and their smiling faces pop into view whenever the screensaver kicks in on my computer. I know the work environment may sometimes dictate otherwise. Some offices truly are not family-friendly, but I find that the charm of a toothless baby smile or my older son's cocky grin will warm the heart of even my most "cool" clients. They look, they smile, a short conversation that is more personal than professional follows, and we are suddenly both more human and, sometimes, even feel an instant bond.

Thoughts of my boys also help lighten my mood on the toughest of workdays. One morning, when my son Will was three years old, I was walking him to his preschool class. As we neared his classroom, he gave me a once over and asked why I was wearing my "fancy suit clothes." I told him I had an important meeting. He looked up at me and asked, "Are you going to dance there?" I laughed and said, "No, I don't think so." He got very serious, looked me straight in the eyes and said, "Well, you should, Mommy." I told him he was right, we really should dance at the meeting. I managed to contain my laughter until he was inside the room. The vision of the Board of Directors dancing around the conference room practically had me rolling on the floor.

His comment kept me smiling through that meeting, and mentioning it to a few of my mom (and even dad) clients has actually resulted in a few quick waltz steps and one great "John Travolta Saturday Night Fever" moment.

Of course, you have to know your audience. In many cases, children create a common bond, but there are also those professionals who do adhere to the philosophy that "work is work and home is home." I don't start conversations with new clients by talking about my children. I usually follow their cues: family photos in their office, or Little League trophies on the desk. Sometimes, the family talk comes out further down the line. Sometimes, it never comes up at all. Yes, I do have clients with whom I work regularly who don't know much about my boys. If they've been with me for a while, they definitely know they exist, but I can sense that they want to focus on the job at hand, and I will not try to convert them.

Just as my boys bring joy to my work days, feeling free to talk about work at home and even letting them see me work during the evening, when necessary, is already having a great influence on the boys. I am not sure they understand exactly what a client is, but they must think a client is something good and nice. The boys regularly pick pretty flowers and leaves in the morning and ask me to give them to my clients. Sometimes, I do!

A small sign near my desk says, "Mothers of little boys work from son up to son down." True. And it can be great fun if you don't divide your time, and truly live one, wonderful life.

33 Education Is a Life-long Journey

Being a single mom, working full time, and going to school two nights a week took some juggling (to say the least).

Katherine Watt is VP of Human Resources for a global high tech company in Silicon Valley and the proud mother of two beautiful and smart young women.

At 18, I was off to college, choosing San Diego State because it was the farthest I could get from home and still be in California (and it had a beach). The following couple years would prove I was no match for the party lifestyle all around me. My "Poli Sci" major and "Econ" minor soon became a major in beach and a minor in boys. While it came as a shock to my poor parents, it was no big surprise to me when I got the letter from school that I was out.

Fast forward eight years, an eternity to a 28-year-old. I was a married, pregnant, bored mom of a one-year-old in a track house in San Jose, CA. In an effort to find some intellectual stimulation, I went back to school. My one-year-old learned to walk in her babysitter's dormitory while I was in class. She had more "friends" on campus than I did! My second baby was cooperatively born Thursday, right after International Law and way before Tuesday's Women in Literature. In three years, I was back on track with a Bachelor's degree.

I was on a roll. I decided to pursue an MBA. Yet, since I was facing a divorce and full-time work, my MBA would be five years away! I would be an ancient 35 by then! When I landed my first administrative job, at $7.50 an hour, I figured I'd be working 40-hour weeks for a long time. I could continue at $7.50 an hour, or I could arm myself with the skills to command something more.

Being a single mom, working full time, and going to school two nights a week took some juggling (to say the least). I quickly found that the advantages far outweighed the costs. By choosing class projects from my work environment, a first-hand application of the theories made the book stuff real, while simultaneously impressing my bosses. I started to see my stock quickly rising in the workplace, and I truly enjoyed what I was learning in the classroom.

I don't want to downplay the finagling it took to make the arrangements for childcare and the impact going to school had on my young daughters. But there were some surprising by-products of this process that surpassed my own goal. MBA programs require a significant amount of group work. When my classmates determined we should meet on Saturdays, it was always an annoyance. My children and I would trudge to the school and find the right classroom. Huge box of chalk in hand, my daughters would find an empty room and create murals on the chalkboards, while I did my meeting thing. The girls spent many happy hours on campus. In their young realities, they went to school when Mom went to school. It was what people do. My daughters became life-long learners.

Today, my oldest daughter is working on her Ph.D. Her sister earned her Bachelor's and is considering going to graduate school. Both girls study things that are just "out there and interesting." The oldest has mastered Spanish and German and the youngest French and Italian.

You may be five or even eight years older at the end of the process. But you will be five or eight years older anyway. Will that time find you with or without those academic credentials? At times, you might wonder if there is a light at the end of the tunnel or just another train. If you keep at it, you will find, as with many things in life, the joy is in the journey. Not the destination.

Observe the Peace

This is what matters, this little person sleeping peacefully in his crib.

Melanie Bertrand is a single mom working full time as a research assistant in a molecular genetics/microbial evolution lab. Her two-year-old son spends week days in daycare and plays all weekend with Mommy.

Every night, the last thing I do before I go to bed is quietly go into my son's room. There, beside his bed, I take a couple deep breaths and listen in the darkness. At first, I can't see anything, but as I quiet myself, I can hear his breathing. Then, slowly, as my eyes adjust, I can make out the stripes of his blanket. I can see him sleeping. I watch and more details resolve themselves. He's relaxed. Bunny's ear lies casually across his wrist; his other hand is flung out and away.

No matter what has been going on, I calm down. This is what matters, this little person sleeping peacefully in his crib. Not the fights I've had with his father, not the stresses at work, not the airline that has lost my luggage, found it, then lost it again. My son is sleeping and is at peace, and that is what is important in my life. I tell this most important little package of life how much I love him, make sure his blanket is tucked around him, and go to bed for what I need: a good night's sleep.

I have memories of my mother doing the same thing. Every night before bed, she would come and "tuck me in." She even did it when I was in high school; I think I asked her to continue. The memories are vague, more of knowing I was loved than what she looked like or what she did. Now, I think, I understand why.

Research has clearly shown that people who meditate are happier than those who do not. Teach someone basic meditation skills, have them practice them for a month, and you can see measurable changes in brain activity patterns relating to happiness using MRIs.

"Yeah, right," you scoff. "What working mother has time to meditate?" Meditation is not limited to sitting in uncomfortable positions, saying "Ooommmm" while listening to a gong. It doesn't need to take hours. Meditation is simply achieving a state of observation, or noticing. When we observe and recognize the good things in life, find gratitude in ourselves, see the positives, we open ourselves to the possibility that, just maybe, things aren't so bad. Writing in a journal, saying grace at dinner, and watching your sleeping baby can all be meditation.

It's so easy to get caught up in the negativity, the stress, the rush of working life. Work has deadlines and petty people. You rush to pick up the kids at daycare, get supper into them, get them bathed and into bed, then steal an hour or so for yourself. You go to sleep thinking about tomorrow's work. The alarm goes off, you rush to get the kids out the door, you kiss a booboo, find your bag, oops, forgot your lunch, off to work!

Break the cycle. End it tonight. Go and watch your child sleep for a couple of minutes. Observe your child. Really listen to those breaths. They might falter, or speed up, for a moment. But notice that they return to their rhythm. Notice how your son or daughter sleeps. And hear your own breathing. Recognize the stress you're feeling and tell it to take a hike, because you're watching your child sleep. Remind yourself that this is what is important in life. You'll be happier for doing this.

And then go get the sleep you need to conquer another day.

35 Don't Buy the Wipe Warmer

Trust me when I tell you that no child on earth has ever failed to thrive as an adult because his excrement was not dabbed gently off his posterior at a delightful 86 degrees Fahrenheit.

Liz Gumbinner is the co-founder and editor of CoolMomPicks.com, the popular shopping and review Web site for parents of young children. She's also a writer and columnist and the author of top parenting blog, Mom-101.

I can't begin to add up the hundreds of hours during my first pregnancy that I dreamingly gazed online at organic knit baby booties and sweated over nursing pillow fabric choices, cross-referencing my selections with recommendations on two different message boards, three baby books, and the suggestions of a half dozen girlfriends.

Oh, the time suck of it all. Surely, I could have put those hours to use writing the great American novel. Two of them. Then, translated them both into Aramaic.

We are busy, we working moms; we spend our lives prioritizing obligations, managing our limited time, striving to be creatures of exceptional efficiency. But when it comes down to browsing those online registries, suddenly all judgment flies out the window, and there we are, frittering four entire hours in the virtual "bath and potty" aisle making sure we have the absolute perfect duck-headed towel.

The truth of the matter is, your baby will somehow, magically get dry, regardless of your choice.

Resist, working mamas of the world! Resist those retailer-created checklists that suggest you simply must—*must*—begin your journey into motherhood in possession of 18-24 bibs, 62 side-snap kimono tees, an entire early reading library and the $200 ergonomic memory foam changing pad originally patented by NASA. I can assure you that even that cornerstone of the nursery, the crib, didn't go used in our household for a good year, and even then only because we felt obliged to justify the cost of it. There's just no guarantee as to what you *need*.

Now, let it be known I have no problem with some degree of frivolity. Those brocade car seat covers can be mighty swanky, and indeed there's a reason that $800 stroller is worth the $800. What makes me crazy are those "must-haves" from retailers that prey on our compromised pregnancy brains, then never make it out of the box: the digital thermometer (doesn't work on newborns); the infant high tops (good luck getting those on); the pacifier sterilizer (Hahahahah!). And, the most absurdly frivolous of them all: The wipes warmer.

Trust me when I tell you that no child on earth has ever failed to thrive as an adult because his excrement was not dabbed gently off his posterior at a delightful 86 degrees Fahrenheit.

While you're at it, go ahead and skip the full body bibs, the bathtub temperature monitors, the fancy white noise machines. You don't need that hat that pulls down over the baby's eyes so he can sleep better. You don't need the giant plush hand that "comforts" your child in bed at night. Don't bother with the childproofing items until you know whether you've got yourself a kid who's more of a light-socket-taster or one who prefers hurling himself full force into the coffee table.

The reality is, you may go back and wish you had one of these items. You may angrily shake your fist at me at 3 a.m. and curse my name, just *knowing* that if you had registered for that giant plush hand, it could have solved all of your child's sleep problems. It could happen. But, it probably won't.

Be careful not to confuse the must-haves with the would-be-nice-to-haves. It will save you immeasurable time, energy and agitation that you could fritter away on baby naming Web sites, instead.

In the end, give yourself permission to forgive yourself when you go and buy all the stupid stuff anyway. Because you are pregnant. And, you are crazy.

36

Be Flexible

Juggling a full life with kids, a spouse, volunteer duties, and an active professional career simply requires flexibility.

Tenny Frost is Executive Director of Alumni Relations at the Haas School of Business at UC Berkeley. Tenny lives in Albany, California, and is married with two children. In 2007, Tenny was recognized as one of the "Top 25 Women Re-defining Success."

"Whatever you do, remember, that the most important thing is to always be flexible...." This was the sage advice my very wise and insightful 102-year-old Baltimore Grandmother always gave me whenever I visited her. She would always weave this comment into our conversation at some point. It would ring in my ears for days after our special visits. That magical phrase "Be Flexible" became a core principle for me after I became a working mother of two beautiful children.

Juggling a full life with kids, a spouse, volunteer duties, and an active professional career simply requires flexibility. If you are not flexible, you can miss out on a lot of things. I would get very frustrated with myself when I got too rigid or stuck in my ways. The solution was to simply relax and try and look at the situation differently. As a result, I truly believe that this core value, being flexible, has allowed me to be successful at work and at home.

At work, making strategic decisions and managing priorities for me and others is a daily requirement. At home, the same skills are applicable. I have discovered that the more I plan, the easier it is to build in options and time so that I *can be flexible*. Now, by default, I find myself planning my work projects with built-in "what if moments." This extra thinking and planning allows me to be more adaptable when things go off track at home or work.

As working moms know, things never go as planned. Kids get sick, but they never seem to get sick on the days that could work well for you! They always get sick on the days that you have a major presentation or event, or, god forbid, a flight out of town for business. I'll never forget the morning my 3-year-old daughter threw up all over herself and her bed as I was on my way out the door for a major work event and a long weekend out of town. My husband and I had planned a trip for our 10-year wedding anniversary. We were leaving the kids behind with the grandparents so that we could jet off to Mexico for a few days (our first major break/vacation since the birth of our kids). My heart sank, as my daughter become more and more ill. Luckily, I was able to shift a few things around and reached out to my staff for help so that I could take it a bit slower that morning at home. I did get to the event, and it went fine. We also got on that plane for Mexico later that night and enjoyed the long weekend together! Slowing down and being flexible made that horrible (and oh so guilty) situation, well, not so horrible anymore.

Another critical part of this guiding principle has been to create a staff environment that embraces flexible work styles and arrangements. Not only do I personally need, want, and desire a flexible work schedule to accomplish my work-life-family balance, but I think it is a very healthy thing to offer everyone (whether or not they have kids!). With today's technology and communication tools, flexible work arrangements are vital to the success of teams and individuals in the workplace. Productivity, respect, and teamwork is on the rise in my workplace as a result.

At home, I have found that as much as I try to map out and plan the week or weekend activities, they are bound to change for the better, and, well, sometimes for the worse. A new idea for fun or family bonding might arise, so "going with the flow" is a theme I try to follow.

I am definitely not perfect at this "being flexible" thing. But, I certainly know that using this as my mantra has kept me focused, happy, and successful over the years.

Children Should Be Loved, Not Managed

... By over-managing my children, I am taking away the very essence of being a child.

Kyra Posma is a 37-year-old wife and mother, married 10 years. She and her husband have two sons ages four and six.

As a mother, I worry about my children's health, safety, and happiness. Additionally, as a working mom, I worry how my work schedule affects them. I work out of necessity and do not allow myself to feel guilty. In fact, I enjoy working and at times I think even if I had a choice, I would still work. I do, on the other hand, make a conscious effort to try to minimize any effect of our daily routine. As we all know, the daily grind can be exhausting, especially for children.

I started to read the book *"Parenting from the Inside Out"* by Daniel J. Siegel, M.D., and Mary Hartzell, M. Ed., and came across the following quote:

"Children need to be enjoyed and valued, not managed."

When I first read this, I thought; "What a powerful statement." As I read it over and over, I realized, the first part is easy. Everyone loves and values their children. The second part is harder.

As a working mom, I thought, how can I not manage them? If I didn't manage them, I would not get to work on time, they wouldn't get to school on time, homework wouldn't get done, dinner wouldn't get made. As I thought about this statement more, I realized that by over-managing my children, I am taking away the very essence of being a child. Rather than letting them play hide-and-seek with me, helping them get dressed, looking at the snow, or even picking out a different shirt, I found myself rushing them.

"Hurry Up, we're running late." "Don't jump on the bed." "Stop fooling around." "Sit down and eat." These are all too familiar phrases heard around our house in the morning. Often, by the time I got to work, I was so frustrated I was ready to explode, and the day was just starting. Imagine, how they felt.

I started getting up earlier. I noticed on the days when I don't rush the children, allow them to enjoy waking up, limit hovering over them to make sure we are keeping to schedule, we all start the day in a better mood. I also notice, on the days that I do rush out of the house, I end up in traffic or behind a school bus anyway. Either way, I end up at work at the same time, so why not make our time pleasurable?

I started to see the rewards of my new approach almost immediately. One day, my son had learned to tie his shoes while at school. The next morning he wanted to show me how he could tie his shoes by himself. Since he just started, he was having problems and it was taking several minutes. Before my new-found attitude, I would have taken over and tied his shoes for him, so we could get in the car. On this day, however, I said to myself "When I get there, I will get there," and, patiently and excitedly, observed him. When he was done, he was so proud of himself, as was I. He went to school proud and excited to show everyone.

The bottom line is time management—of your time, not your children's. Give yourself the time to enjoy being with your children while they are growing up. Cherish those great experiences and create the magical memories. Make sure to give yourself enough time so you allow your children the time to be just that, children. Their agenda is completely different than ours, and if we valued them, we would allocate our time so that we can honor what is important to them, being a child. I now find that I enjoy being one with them.

38 Play the Question Game

They can recite entire conversations that occurred during the day word for word if it is important for their answer.

Nancy Erba is a single working mother with two beautiful smart children and an extremely supportive family. She is a vice president at a major storage company in Silicon Valley.

If you are like me, it's sometimes hard to have an in-depth conversation with your kids. The answer to "How was your day today?" is often met with "fine," "good," "ok." When asked, "Did anything special happen today?" the answer is "No, not really." You get the idea. I also struggle with how to talk to them about my day, without diving into details about a frustrating meeting, or a particularly successful project. It's very important to me to teach them about my career. It is a very important part of my life and who I am as a person.

I stumbled upon something that works for my family a little bit by accident, but it's now become one of our favorite bedtime rituals. We don't do it every day, sometimes only once a week, but more times than not, it will be one of my kids who says, "Hey Mom, let's play the question game!" when getting ready for bed.

I think the game started one Sunday night during a particularly busy weekend as a way to reconnect and settle down before bedtime. I wanted to see what activities they liked best and what, maybe, wasn't so high on their list. The game goes something like this: "What made you feel happy today?" The answers range from "We went out for ice cream for dessert" to "I got 100 percent on my spelling test" or "It's Friday!"

I quickly learned two things. First, this was an awesome way to learn things about what my children were feeling without asking them very pointed questions and putting them on the spot. Second, their minds are capable of retaining an amazing amount of information. They can recite entire conversations that occurred during the day, word for word, if it is important for their answer. Over time, our questions have evolved to quite an extensive list:

- "When did you feel angry/frustrated/disappointed today?"
- "What made you laugh today?"
- "What made you feel proud today?"
- "Tell me something nice you saw someone else do today."
- "Tell me something nice you did for someone else today."
- "What/who hurt your feelings today?"

It's a very low-key way to start a conversation. I learn a lot about what happens at school, at sports events or during play dates. When something happens that makes them sad or hurts their feelings, we talk about it and how to address it and move forward the next day. The question game also encourages the kids to think about what events make them feel certain ways and how their actions affect other people. I always try to include the "What made you feel proud today?" question, so that they have an opportunity to share something they might not otherwise have told me and to give me a chance to tell them how very proud I am of them, too.

There has been an interesting unintended outcome of this little game; they want to ask me questions, too! This gives me a chance to talk to them about what happened in my day. It brings them a little closer to what I do at work every day. I'll give examples of things I'm proud of, of things that went really well at work, and also situations that might be frustrating to me. This gives me an opportunity to reinforce important messages like: how important education is; how I hope they will explore lots of different activities and find a job someday that they really enjoy, too; that adults have good days and bad days at work, just as they do; that I like my job and work really hard at it.

It was really easy to answer the question "What makes you feel proud, Mom?" I told them that, of course, I was very proud of them, but that I am also very proud of my career and being able to share it with them.

39 It's OK to Lie (Sometimes)

If the world is going to pretend I don't have kids, I am going to have imaginary clients.

Michelle Lamar is a mother, wife, marketing geek and author. Michelle writes a parenting blog called "White Trash Mom" and wrote the book White Trash Mom Handbook (August 2008). Michelle lives with her two daughters, ages 10 and 14, and her husband Tim.

I tried to be a perfect mother. I tried to do it "all," because I thought that was what I was supposed to do. Then, one day, I woke up and realized that it was completely insane to try to *think* I could do it all. Something had to give. In my case, I had to get creative with the truth.

I worked in sales for years at an ad agency. Along the way, I became a mother of two girls…and a pathological liar. To manufacture more time and flexibility in order to take kids to appointments, do work at their school, I made up a fake client. It made it easier for me to keep track of because lying is much more difficult than telling the truth. It became a "code" for my co-workers (the women, of course) that I was on a "child duty" when I left the office. I would tell my co-workers that I was going to see *"Charlie"* over at *"Corporate Solutions"* for a meeting.

At the mention of *"Charlie"* or the *"Corporate Solutions"* meeting, my friends would know that one of the girls had to go to the doctor, or that I had playground duty at school. The code also kept them alert, so if a problem came up while I was at *"Charlie's,"* they could call me on my cell. I can't tell you how many work problems I took care of while on playground duty at my kids' school.

I know lying is sad and twisted. So is the fact that there are no good childcare options for families here in the United States, one of the richest countries in the world.

We are on our own to figure out how to care for our children and make a living. Did you know that:

* 70 percent of Moms with children under 18 work. A recent study by Harvard and McGill Universities ranks the U.S. at the bottom of the world's nations in terms of providing a safety net for Moms and children?

* Of the 52 million working parents in the United States, it is estimated that between $50 billion and $300 billion dollars are lost every year because of lost job productivity due to parents being worried and stressed about their children in after-school care or without proper care after school.

Since the modern workplace pretends that my children don't exist, and this isn't going to change anytime soon, *I am working around it.* If the world is going to pretend I don't have kids, I am going to have imaginary clients.

You can read more of my tips on how to keep sane in my book, *The White Trash Mom Handbook.*

40 Don't Forget to Lock The Door

... Maintaining a satisfying and loving relationship with your husband is exhausting.

Kelli Glass is in transition from stay-at-home to work-at-home mom. She is a transplanted Texan and lives in California with her husband and two boys.

Before kids (BK), you had time for yourself and for your husband: quiet evenings at home, discussing politics or the latest movie over a bottle of wine, or dinner and dancing at your favorite restaurant. I'm talking about romance, spending hours in bed on a Sunday morning reading the paper and sharing some special "alone time any time" with your husband. Remember those days?

After kids (AK), you're working all day in an office or in the home, or both. You are queen of multi-tasking: folding laundry while you're on a conference call, helping with homework while you check e-mail, driving the kids to and from their activities while quizzing them on spelling words, cleaning the bathroom while bathing your children. You get the picture. At the end of the day, what do you really want to do? The kids are asleep in bed, the dishes are washed and put away, e-mail is under control for the moment, the lights are low and for the first time that day, you are alone with your husband. BK: the answer is easy, there isn't even a question. AK: falling asleep on the couch or reading a novel might top the list of things to do, with "sleeping with husband" being number five or six.

Does this make you a bad wife? I don't think so. It means you're like most other working moms. The choice of going to bed to sleep rather than sleeping with your husband identifies you as a busy person, with a busy life and very little time to yourself. And that's ok.

Life is exhausting, work is exhausting, keeping a family thriving is exhausting, and maintaining a satisfying and loving relationship with your husband is exhausting. Yet, your life (at home and at work), family and marital relationships are all entwined and equally important. You can't have one without the other.

I believe the key to marital success AK is to find the proper balance between the three—life, family and marriage. One solution is to change your outlook. A date with your husband doesn't have to mean a babysitter and a night on the town. It can be a quiet evening at home, a picnic in the living room after the kids have gone to bed. Employ your best problem-solving techniques. Tell your husband how much it turns you on when he empties the dishwasher or takes out the trash. You'll get the extra help with the housework, and he'll get a thrill knowing his domestic skills excite you. Engage in creative scheduling and meet for a quick lunch at home while the kids are at school. Or, set a date to meet in bed at 10 p.m. one evening. Put the date on your calendar and his calendar, and you'll both have something to look forward to at the end of the day.

If you are successful in your problem-solving and inventive scheduling techniques, then you and your husband will be able to share romantic trysts reminiscent of BK. A word of warning, however: do not let this accomplishment go to your head. You still have children and still need to take the necessary precautions to protect you and your husband's privacy. A good friend of mine and her husband were taking advantage of their creative scheduling early one morning, when they were surprised by their child at the edge of the bed. When asked what they were doing, my friend's husband replied that he and Mommy were "naked wrestling." Fortunately, junior was satisfied with this answer. In fact, he asked if he could join in the fun! Did I mention that a sense of humor was also necessary to maintaining your romantic life AK—that and a good lock on the bedroom door!

41

Dads Make Great Parents, Too

As a SAHD, your husband works fulltime, too.

Jamie Hayden is a copywriter and the working mom behind ParenTeam.com, an online resource for working wives of SAHD's. A mother of two and the wife of a SAHD for over a decade, Jamie loves talking to others about the rewards of this unique lifestyle.

As the working wife of a stay-at-home dad (SAHD), I can tell you first-hand that some people just don't know what to make of them ... "Does he go to Mommy & Me classes?" "Has he always had a fondness for cleaning and grocery shopping?" "Why doesn't he have a real job?"

Through the years, I've come to realize that the quizzical looks, blank stares and not-so-polite comments are part of SAHD territory. Yet, the truth is, that dads make great parents, too. To be sure, transitioning to a SAHD household isn't easy. It's often fraught with discord and burnt macaroni and cheese along the way. However, the important thing is to keep your eyes on the prize—the little ones you brought into this world.

My husband and I re-arranged our lives ten years ago to create more balance for ourselves and our two children. We function as a team, complete with family meetings and chore lists. After all, when you're a working mom and your husband is a SAHD, gender roles are less defined. Traditional roles become blurry. Operating as a team is a great way to stay connected, maintain communication, and promote a positive sense of family.

As a working mom, you hold a full-time job. As a SAHD, your husband works fulltime, too. For you, ultimate success comes down to:

- Understanding that your husband does not work for you and is not your personal assistant.
- Respecting his approach to discipline and other parental responsibilities (especially, if they are a bit different from yours).
- Realizing that life will go on whether he stores the yogurts on the second shelf of the refrigerator or the first.
- Maintaining the control to realize that you're not in control of what happens inside your home every day—and being okay with that.
- *Never* taking him for granted.

Naturally, not all men are cut out for the SAHD life. But if yours is, by all means embrace it if you can. At the end of the day, the benefits can be significant. The accolades and cheers I often hear are music to my ears—and the extra push I sometimes need to get through my day.

Indeed, you can be confident knowing that while you're at work, he's bandaging the boo-boos, preparing the meals, wiping up the spills—and your children—and generally running the show. What's more, he's cheering them on at their baseball games, rooting for them at their ice skating championships, and helping them determine what "x" and "y" equals in time for the algebra test. That speaks volumes.

Just last week, a working friend of mine with a stay-at-home husband came home after a long day behind the desk to find him immersed in a backyard water balloon fight with their three children. "They hardly noticed me at all," she complained later to me. "Nobody came over to say hello or to ask me about my day."

At that very moment, I mounted my soapbox and congratulated my friend. "Your husband is a great success! He's swimming upstream against the stereotype of what a stay-at-home parent ought to be. He's carving a gratifying life out of being the best hands-on parent he can be. And he's building incredible relationships with your children."

What is the bottom line? Now is a great time to be part of a SAHD family. Grab a water balloon and join in the fun.

These Are Our Rules. What Are Yours?

Being a working mom is a mixed blessing.

So, what do you think? Are you nodding in agreement? Or, do you think we're all crazy and don't understand your world? Agree or disagree, we invite you to become part of the conversation.

Being a working mom is a mixed blessing. No one but another working mom understands how hard it is to keep yourself together during a big meeting while your child is at home throwing up. These rules are the collective knowledge of a lot of caring, experienced, and giving women who want other moms to learn from their successes and, sometimes, their failures.

What works for you? Let other working moms know on our blog at:
http://42rules.com/working_moms.
We're looking forward to hearing from you—in your spare time.

About the Author

Laura Lowell has navigated the waters of working motherhood since the birth of her first daughter in 2000. Part-time, full-time and entrepreneur—she has tried it all. In the process, she came to meet, question, and learn from other working moms. *42 Rules for Working Moms* shares those experiences with others.

Prior to launching Impact Marketing Group, Laura was the Director, Worldwide Consumer Marketing Communications for Hewlett-Packard, where she was responsible for planning and implementing integrated marketing campaigns across all HP consumer product lines. Early in her career, Laura spent several years at Intel Corporation, where she was on the start-up team that developed and implemented the Intel Inside® branding program.

Laura's degree in International Relations prepared her for work assignments in Hong Kong and London, after which she received her MBA from UC Berkeley's Haas School of Business, with an emphasis on marketing and entrepreneurship. She lives in Los Gatos, California, with her husband, Rick, and their two daughters age 6 and 8.

$1 from the sale of each book will benefit *Dress for Success Worldwide* (http://www.dressforsuccess.org), a non-profit organization whose mission is to promote the economic independence of disadvantaged women by providing professional attire, a network of support, and the career development tools to help them thrive in work and in life.

Write Your Own Rules

You can write your own 42 Rules book, and we can help you do it—from initial concept, to writing and editing, to publishing and marketing. If you have a great idea for a 42 Rules book, then we want to hear from you.

As you know, the books in the 42 Rules series are practical guidebooks that focus on a single topic. The books are written in an easy-to-read format that condenses the fundamental elements of the topic into 42 Rules. They use realistic examples to make their point and are fun to read.

Two Kinds of 42 Rules Books

42 Rules books are published in two formats: the single-author book and the contributed-author book. The single-author book is a traditional book written by one author. The contributed-author book (like *42 Rules for Working Moms*) is a compilation of Rules, each written by a different contributor, which support the main topic. If you want to be the sole author of a book or one of its contributors, we can help you succeed!

42 Rules Program

A lot of people would like to write a book, but only a few actually do. Finding a publisher, and distributing and marketing the book are challenges that prevent even the most ambitious of authors to ever get started.

At 42 Rules, we help you focus on and be successful in the writing of your book. Our program concentrates on the following tasks so you don't have to:

- **Publishing:** You receive expert advice and guidance from the Executive Editor, copy editors, technical editors, and cover and layout designers to help you create your book.

- **Distribution:** We distribute your book through the major book distribution channels, like Baker & Taylor and Ingram, Amazon.com, Barnes and Noble, Borders Books, etc.

- **Marketing:** 42 Rules has a full-service marketing program that includes a customized Web page for you and your book, email registrations and campaigns, blogs, webcasts, media kits and more.

Whether you are writing a single-authored book or a contributed-author book, you will receive editorial support from 42 Rules Executive Editor, Laura Lowell, author of *42 Rules of Marketing*, which was rated Top 5 in Business Humor and Top 25 in Business Marketing on Amazon.com (December 2007), and author and Executive Editor of *42 Rules for Working Moms*.

Accepting Submissions

If you want to be a successful author, we'll provide you the tools to help make it happen. Start today by answering the following questions and visit our website at http://superstarpress.com/ for more information on submitting your 42 Rules book idea.

Super Star Press is now accepting submissions for books in the 42 Rules book series. For more information, email info@superstarpress.com or call 408-257-3000.

Other Happy About Books

Dignity Rocks!

This unique book opens up discussions on dignity, self-respect, and other sometimes difficult topics to express for children.

Paperback $19.95
eBook $11.95

Lessons About Life Momma Never Taught Us

For every modern girl to take care of herself and to learn to manage her relationships, her attitude, and her life.

Paperback $14.95
eBook $11.95

30day Bootcamp:
Your Ultimate Life Makeover

A step-by-step program
that will teach you all the
tips, tricks, and techniques
you need to get back in the
driver's seat of your life.

Paperback $19.95
eBook $11.95

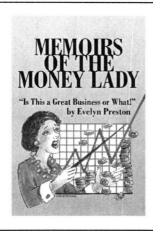

Memoirs of the Money Lady

This must-read empowers
women to handle their own
finances and to learn that
dealing with money does
not have to be a difficult or
unhappy task.

Paperback $19.95
eBook $11.95

Rule #1: Stop Talking!
A Guide to Listening

Learn to become a savvy,
critical listener and listen to
yourself to create the life
you truly want.

Paperback $16.95
eBook $11.95

Happy About Animals

An 8-year old's perspective
on sharing the Earth.

Paperback $19.95
eBook $11.95

Purchase these books at Happy About
http://happyabout.info
or at other online and physical bookstores.

A Message From Super Star Press™

Thank you for your purchase of this 42 Rules Series book. It is available online at:
http://happyabout.info/42rules/workingmoms.php or at other online and physical bookstores. To learn more about contributing to books in the 42 Rules series, check out http://superstarpress.com.

Super Star Press™ is interested in you if you are an author who would like to submit a non-fiction book proposal or a corporation that would like to have a book written for you. Please contact us by email info@superstarpress.com or phone (408-257-3000).

Please contact us for quantity discounts at sales@superstarpress.com

If you want to be informed by email of upcoming books, please email bookupdate@superstarpress.com.

LaVergne, TN USA
18 November 2009
164495LV00004B/6/P

9 780979 942846